PRAISE FOR MATT FITZGERALD
AND HIS FITNESS BOOKS

"Fitzgerald is going to go down as one of the most competent and prolific authors of books for serious runners covering just about every legitimate aspect of the all-important runner's lifestyle."

—LetsRun.com

"If you're looking to get to your peak performance weight or explore the mind-body connection of running, writer Matt Fitzgerald has some advice for you. . . . Fitzgerald, an expert in endurance training and nutrition, explores a wide range of topics and cutting-edge developments from the world of running and endurance sports."

—ESPN.com

"Sports nutritionist Matt Fitzgerald lets us in on his no-diet secrets that can help endurance athletes get leaner, stronger, and faster."

—*Men's Fitness*

"The elements and philosophy laid out in *Run* were fundamental and played an essential role in my overall success throughout my career as a self-coached athlete."

—Alan Culpepper, 2000 and 2004 U.S. Olympian, sub-four-minute miler, sub–2:10 marathoner

"Extremely well-done . . . a must for marathoners!"

—*Library Journal*

"In his latest book, Matt Fitzgerald successfully explains the mind-body method of running. . . . Anyone trying to improve and realize their true running potential should read *Run*."

—Kara Goucher, 2008 Olympian and world championship medalist

continued . . .

T0002750

"Amateur to professional athletes can optimize their potential with this book." —Bike World News

Racing Weight answers the difficult questions athletes often have about dieting, including how to handle the off-season. The book gives readers a scientifically backed system to discover your optimum race weight, as well as five steps to achieve it." —*Triathlete*

"You will gain valuable information and insight about how to fuel your body from this book." —Portland Book Review

80/20 RUNNING

RUN STRONGER AND RACE FASTER BY TRAINING SLOWER

Matt Fitzgerald

NEW AMERICAN LIBRARY

New American Library
Published by the Penguin Group
Penguin Group (USA) LLC, 375 Hudson Street,
New York, New York 10014

USA | Canada | UK | Ireland | Australia | New Zealand | India | South Africa | China
penguin.com
A Penguin Random House Company

First published by New American Library,
a division of Penguin Group (USA) LLC

First Printing, September 2014

LIBRARY OF CONGRESS CATALOGING-IN-PUBLICATION DATA:
Fitzgerald, Matt.
80/20 running: run stronger and race faster by training slower/Matt Fitzgerald.
p. cm.
ISBN 978-0-451-47088-1 (paperback)
1. Sports—Physiological aspects. 2. Exercise. 3. Physical fitness. I. Title. II. Title: Eighty-twenty running.
RC1235.F58 2014
613.7'1—dc23   2014015921

Printed in the United States of America

23rd Printing

Set in ITC New Baskerville Std
Designed by Pauline Neuwirth

CONTENTS

FOREWORD

Fifteen years ago, when I was training at a high level with my twin brother, Weldon, a twenty-eight-minute 10K runner, and dreaming of the U.S. Olympic Trials, I had a conversation with my beloved ninety-year-old grandmother, "BB," that I'll never forget.

"Boys, I don't understand this running thing," she said. "I can imagine nothing worse than waking up and realizing I was going to have to run fifteen miles that day."

"BB, it's not like you think," I replied. "Running is the best part of my day. Most of the time I'm not running hard. Weldon and I just run side by side at a relaxed pace and carry on a conversation for an hour and a half. It's a ninety-minute social hour."

"Oh, that doesn't sound too bad," BB said. "I always viewed running as a form of grueling punishment."

My grandmother's misconception was far from uncommon. A lot of people viewed running as she did—and still do. But Matt Fitzgerald is about to let you in on a secret: Running isn't always supposed to be hard. In fact, most of the time, it should be easy and enjoyable.

You see, in order to yield steady improvement, a training system must be repeatable—day after day, week after week, month after month. And guess what. Hard running isn't repeatable, either physically or psychologically. If you do too much of it, your body will burn out if your mind doesn't first.

The ultimate compliment for me in my peak training years was being passed on my easy runs by a runner who had a marathon time more than an hour slower than mine. I'd say to myself, "He's wearing himself out today. I'm building myself up."

All too many runners wear themselves out by running too fast too often—now more than ever. There is an obsession these days with high intensity. Most of the trendy new training systems are focused on speed work. Running magazines, Web sites, and books can't say enough about the magical power of intervals. Even champion runners are more likely to credit their speed work instead of their easy running when interviewed after winning a race. Yet the typical elite runner does eight miles of easy running for every two miles of faster running.

Speed work may be "sexier" than easy running, but just as a weight lifter doesn't go hard two days in a row, a runner shouldn't either. A weight lifter actually gets stronger on days off. Similarly, a runner gets faster by going slow in the majority of his or her runs. Strangely, most weight lifters seem to understand this principle, while most recreationally competitive runners don't. Too much hard running is the most common mistake in the sport.

Thanks to Matt Fitzgerald's truly groundbreaking 80/20 running program, that's about to change. Building on new science that *proves* that a "mostly-slow" training approach is more effective, *80/20 Running* makes the number one training secret of the world's best runners available to runners of all abilities and all levels of experience. I only wish this book had existed when I was competing. As much as I appreciated the value of slow running, Fitzgerald's 80/20 running program makes optimal training simpler and more reproducible than it's ever been by boiling it all down to one basic rule: Do 80 percent of your running at low intensity and the other 20 percent at moderate to high intensity. The rest is details.

I know it might be hard to believe that you can actually race faster by training slower, but after you read the compelling case for Fitzgerald's new method, you will definitely think it's worth a try. And once you've tried it, I guarantee you will be completely convinced. If 80/20 running doesn't make your race times faster and your running experience more enjoyable—well, then I guess my grandma BB was right about running after all!

—Robert Johnson, cofounder of LetsRun.com

80/20 RUNNING

INTRODUCTION

Do you want to run faster? Then you need to slow down.

As contradictory as it may seem, the secret to becoming a speedier runner is going slow most of the time. The key difference between runners who realize their full potential and those who fall short is the amount of slow running that each group does. Recent analyses of the world's best runners—the first studies to rigorously assess how these athletes really train—have revealed that they spend about four-fifths of their total training time below the *ventilatory threshold* (VT), or running slow enough to carry on a conversation. New research also suggests that nonelite runners in the "recreationally competitive" category improve most rapidly when they take it easy in training more often than not.

The vast majority of runners, however, seldom train at a truly comfortable intensity. Instead, they push themselves a little day after day, often without realizing it. If the typical elite runner does four easy runs for every hard run, the average recreationally competitive runner—and odds are, you're one of them—does just one easy run for every hard run. Simply put: Running too hard too often is the single most common and detrimental mistake in the sport.

As mistakes go, this one is pretty understandable. Going fast in training makes intuitive sense to most runners. After all, the purpose of training is to prepare for races, and the purpose of racing is to see how fast you can reach the finish line. Nobody denies that running fast in training is important, but as I will show you in this book, runners who strictly limit their faster running in workouts derive more benefit from these sessions and perform better in races, whereas those who go overboard end up training in a state of constant fatigue that limits their progress.

I myself learned this lesson the hard way. I started running a few weeks before my twelfth birthday. My first run was a six miler on dirt roads surrounding my family's home in rural New Hampshire. I wore a stopwatch and pushed to get a good time—ideally, something relatively close to my dad's usual time for the same route. Two days later, I repeated the workout, aiming to improve my performance, which I was able to do. Two days later, I took another crack at lowering my mark and succeeded again.

Young and naive as I was, I expected this pattern of steady gains to continue indefinitely. After a few weeks, though, I was no longer improving. I was also feeling lousy on all of my runs, and the joy had gone out of them. Eventually I quit training and turned my athletic focus back to soccer.

A couple of years later, I blew out a knee on the soccer field. After recovering from surgery, I decided to start running again. As chance would have it, one of the coaches at my high school was Jeff Johnson, a brilliant mentor of young runners who had the distinction of being Nike's first employee and the man who named the company. Jeff's coaching philosophy was heavily influenced by that of Arthur Lydiard, a New Zealander who had revolutionized the sport in 1960 with a method that featured lots of slow, comfortable running and modest amounts of speed work. I thrived on this approach, becoming an All-State performer in cross-country and track and leading my team to a handful of state championship titles.

The secret of slow running is not new. Every winner of a major international competition since the Lydiard revolution of the 1960s owes his or her success to slow running. Despite this fact, only a small fraction of runners today recognizes and exploits the power of slow running. The failure of the "mostly-slow" method to reach all corners of the sport has several causes, one of which is—or *was*—scientific skepticism. While many scientists still believe that slow running is rather useless, there is a revolution happening in the study of the optimal training intensity distribution in running, and the new advocates of slow running are looking like winners.

Previously, scientists who dismissed slow running as "junk miles" seemed to have the weight of evidence on their side. Then along came Stephen Seiler, an American exercise physiologist based in Norway whose intuition told him that the training methods used by the most successful athletes were probably a better representation of what really works than were the limited lab experiments that appeared to suggest that the world's greatest long-distance racers had no idea what they were doing. This intuition led Seiler to embark on a research agenda that culminated in the most significant breakthrough in running since Arthur Lydiard's original discovery of slow running: the 80/20 Rule.

Seiler started by exhaustively analyzing the training methods of world-class rowers and cross-country skiers. He found a remarkable consistency: Athletes in both sports did approximately 80 percent of their training sessions at low intensity and 20 percent at high intensity. In subsequent research, Seiler learned that elite cyclists, swimmers, triathletes, rowers, and—yes—runners did the same thing. Knowing this pattern could not possibly be an arbitrary coincidence, Seiler and other researchers designed studies where athletes were placed on either an 80/20 training regimen or a regimen with more hard training and less easy training. In every case, the results have been the same: 80/20 training yields drastically better results than more intense training.

The 80/20 Rule promises to revolutionize running (and other endurance sports) in a couple of ways. First, it ends the debate over whether a mostly-slow approach or a speed-based approach to training is more effective. No longer will scientists and coaches with a bias for high intensity (or even moderate intensity) be able to steer runners in the wrong direction. Second, by supplying clear numerical targets, Seiler's discovery makes effective training easier even for runners who are already training more or less the right way. The 80/20 Rule removes the guesswork from the training process. Reaping its benefits is a simple matter of planning your workouts in accordance with the rule and monitoring your running intensity during each workout to ensure you're where you're supposed to be.

Seiler's rule also helps runners by explicitly defining low intensity. The boundary between low intensity and moderate intensity, according to Seiler, falls at the ventilatory threshold, which is the intensity level at which the breathing rate abruptly deepens. This threshold is slightly below the more familiar lactate threshold, which you can think of as the highest running intensity at which you can talk comfortably. In well-trained runners, the ventilatory threshold typically falls between 77 percent and 79 percent of maximum heart rate. In pace terms, if your 10K race time is 50 minutes (8:03 per mile), your ventilatory threshold will likely correspond to a pace of 8:40 per mile. If your 10K time is 40 minutes (6:26 per mile), you will probably hit your VT at approximately 7:02 per mile. In either case, running at or below these threshold speeds will feel quite comfortable.

Scientists have determined that the average recreationally competitive runner spends less than 50 percent of his or her total training time at low intensity. This is a problem, because research has also demonstrated that even a 65/35 intensity breakdown yields worse race results than does full compliance with the 80/20 Rule. The good news is that, unless you are an elite runner, it is almost certain that you are doing less than 80 percent of your training at low intensity and that you can improve significantly by slowing down. The purpose of this book is to help you do just that.

When Jeff Johnson showed me the power of slow running during my high school years, I never would have guessed that I would one day coach runners myself. My role is not to innovate and discover, like Arthur Lydiard and Stephen Seiler, but to serve as a link between the innovators and discoverers and the broader running community. Early in my career, I was struck by some of the new ways that elite runners were using cross-training to elevate their performance and avoid injuries, so I wrote *Runner's World Guide to Cross-Training*. Later I developed an interest in how brain science was influencing the sport at the highest level, so I made these new methods available to all in *Brain Training for Runners*.

When I learned about Stephen Seiler's work, I was experienced enough to know immediately that the 80/20 Rule was a game changer. Even though I had always taught a mostly-slow training approach, I was aware that many of my runners ran too hard too often anyway. What I've realized—and what science proves—is that running slow just doesn't come naturally to most runners. The same instinct that I had as an eleven-year-old new runner exists also within countless other runners of all experience levels. It's an impulse to make every run "count" by pushing beyond the level of total comfort. This instinct makes a lot of runners rather hard to coach. It's one thing to give a runner a training plan that is dominated by low-intensity workouts; it is quite another thing for that same runner to actually stay below the ventilatory threshold in all of those designated "easy" runs. I have discovered that unless a runner is systematically held back, he will more often than not run too hard on easy days and unwittingly sabotage his training plan.

Until I found the work of Stephen Seiler, my efforts to keep runners from making the most common mistake in the sport were ineffective. This quickly changed once I studied Seiler's published research as well as that of other leading scientists of the 80/20 revolution. I also made direct contact with Seiler and his collaborators to learn more from them. I began to use the quantitative benchmarks of the 80/20 method to ensure that the training plans I created for runners were neither too hard nor too easy and that workouts were executed correctly. I later designed a range of ready-made 80/20 training plans for the PEAR Mobile app, which uses my voice to guide runners through heart rate–based workouts, and developed a separate 80/20 Running app that keeps track of time spent at low and moderate to high intensities.

Not surprisingly, many runners have had to slow down to conform to my 80/20 guidelines. Some have done so reluctantly, finding it difficult to believe that going easier in training could make them go faster in races. But the runners who have taken a leap of faith and seen the process through have been well rewarded. Their runs have become more pleasant and less draining. They now carry less fatigue from one run to the next and they perform (and feel) better in the few runs that are intended to be faster. Suddenly, it no longer seems impossible to run an extra five or ten miles each week. The ones who take advantage of this opportunity improve even more.

A typical case is Joe from San Diego. An experienced runner and triathlete, Joe had been chasing a sub-three-hour marathon for nearly twenty years when I began to work with him. Previously Joe had been self-coached, and like almost all self-coached runners, he did a lot more moderate-intensity training and a lot less low-intensity training than he thought he did. Getting him to slow down was a challenge. While Joe accepted the 80/20 philosophy in principle, out on the road he kept reverting to old habits. At last, with the help of the PEAR Mobile app, I got Joe to slow down. When he did, his energy level skyrocketed, and we were able to put that energy to good use by adding a few extra miles to his training schedule. In May 2012, at the age of forty-seven, Joe completed the Orange County Marathon in 2:59:20.

Now it's your turn. The purpose of this book is to help you in the same way I have helped runners like Joe since I joined the 80/20 revolution. I will show you how to break the bad habit of running too hard too often and embrace running slow. I will also make the case for 80/20 running by exploring how this method evolved naturally over a period of many decades at the elite level of the sport and analyzing the cutting-edge scientific proof that 80/20 running is more effective than other methods for runners of all experience and ability levels. I will explain *how* 80/20 running maximizes both fitness and running skill. In chapters 6 through 13, I will tell you everything you need to know to practice 80/20 running most effectively.

I am confident that the educational first part of this book will leave you eager to begin using the practical guidelines of the second half. After all, how often do you get to hear that the easier way is the better way?

LEARNING TO SLOW DOWN

A couple of years ago, I designed a custom training plan for a runner named Juan Carlos. He had been running for three years and was frustrated by a recent lack of progress. His 10K PR of 52:30 was showing troubling signs of permanence, and on his training runs, he was lately feeling lousy more often than not. "I can barely run 8:45 [per mile] pace anymore," he told me via e-mail.

I explained to Juan Carlos that, at his current level of fitness, he had no business running 8:45 per mile except in designated moderate-intensity runs, which should have a small place in his training. A pace of 9:30 per mile would be more appropriate for easy runs, I told him, and these should account for about four out of every five runs he did.

Juan Carlos is not the first runner I've had to put the brakes on. In fact, nearly all of the runners who come to me for help are doing their "easy" runs faster than they should. It is also very common for runners to resist the edict to run slower. Many of them just find it hard to believe that slowing down in training will enable them to run faster in races. Juan Carlos sure did. More than once, after I had gotten him started on 80/20 running, he contacted me with questions like "Is it okay if I run faster on days when I feel really good?" Each time I counseled restraint and patience.

80/20 running is very simple. It has two components: planning and monitoring. The planning component entails creating or choosing a training plan that is based on the 80/20 Rule. In other words, the plan should be set up so that roughly 80 percent of your total training time is spent at low intensity (below the ventilatory threshold) and the other 20 percent is spent at moderate to high intensity. The monitoring component entails measuring intensity during each run to ensure you are executing your 80/20 plan correctly.

If you plan and monitor according to the simple guidelines I will present in later chapters, you will soon run better than you ever have. But there's an important first step that you must take before you dive into 80/20 running, and that is embracing the "mostly-slow" approach. This acceptance of slower running needs to occur on two levels: in your mind and in your body.

Embracing 80/20 running mentally means that you are convinced intellectually that it works better than other training methods. I will present all the necessary evidence to show the clear and persuasive merits of 80/20 running in chapters 2 through 5. Embracing 80/20 running in your body means learning to slow down, which many runners, including Juan Carlos, find surprisingly challenging at the beginning, like removing a favorite junk food from the diet. Breaking the habit of pushing yourself during training runs takes some time, so I encourage you to get started right away, even as you continue to read about the 80/20 method. In this chapter, I will show you how to take this first step. Let me begin, though, by explaining why it can be so hard (initially) to run easy.

CAUGHT IN THE MIDDLE

Suppose I were to ask you to put down this book right now and run five miles at your choice of pace, but without wearing a watch. Chances are you would settle into a pace very close to the pace at which you did your last "easy" run, and the one before that, and the one before that. Odds are as well that this pace would put you above the ventilatory threshold, in the moderate-intensity zone.

There are really two problems here. The first issue is that your habitual running pace is doing to you what it did to Juan Carlos: hindering your progress. The second issue is that this pace is *habitual*. It feels natural and has become as familiar as your stride itself through experience. For this reason, your habitual running pace carries inertial force—like all habits, it is hard to break.

Science confirms my observation that most runners push themselves in training most of the time. In 1993, Muriel Gilman of Arizona State University's Exercise and Sport Science Institute handed out heart rate monitors to a group of recreationally competitive female runners and asked them to wear the devices through one week of training. When the week was up, the researchers collected the monitors and calculated how much time the runners had spent in each of three intensity zones.

Gilman placed the border between low and moderate intensity at the ventilatory threshold, which for the women in this study occurred at 82 percent of maximum heart rate. The border between moderate and high intensity was placed at the lactate threshold, which is the exercise intensity at which lactate—an intermediate product of aerobic metabolism—begins to accumulate in the blood. For Gilman's subjects, this threshold occurred at 94 percent of maximum heart rate.

It turned out that, on average, the runners spent 45.8 percent of their total training time for the week at low intensity, an almost identical 45.7 percent at moderate intensity, and the remaining 8.9 percent at high intensity. Other research, which I will detail in later chapters, has shown that runners who balance their training in this way experience far less improvement than runners who perform 80 percent of their running at low intensity and the remaining 20 percent at moderate to high intensity. So it's fair to assume that the roughly 50/50 training approach of

the women in the ASU study—which is the norm for recreationally competitive runners—was holding them back.

Why do most runners spend so much time running at moderate intensity?

The discoverer of the 80/20 Rule, Stephen Seiler, found the
reason may be that, unlike other forms of exercise, running has
a minimum threshold of intensity. Very slow running is not running at all but walking. The average person naturally transitions
from walking to running at a pace of roughly thirteen minutes
per mile. If you start off at a slow walk and gradually increase
your speed, you will find yourself feeling an urge to transition to
running somewhere near that pace. Likewise, if you start off running and gradually slow down, you'll find yourself wanting to
transition to walking at about thirteen minutes per mile.

The problem is that many runners, especially new and over-
weight runners, are already near the ventilatory threshold as
soon as they transition from walking to running. These runners
don't have much room to work within the low-intensity zone. In
contrast, an elite male runner can cruise along at an exhilarating
pace of six minutes per mile and still be well below his ventilatory
threshold. The elite's low-intensity running zone is much broader,
so he naturally spends less time outside it.

This explanation makes a lot of sense, but it does not completely account for the tendency of recreational runners to spend
so much less of their total training time at low intensity than elite
runners do. There is no equivalent of the walk-run transition in
other aerobic activities, such as cycling. Yet, when Belgian researchers measured self-selected exercise intensity in a group of
bicycle commuters, they found that these people chose an intensity that placed them slightly above the ventilatory threshold, just
as recreational runners do. The same phenomenon has also been
observed in swimming and elliptical training—pretty much any
form of aerobic exercise you can name. So the question remains:
Why do most runners instinctively train largely at moderate intensity when training mostly at low intensity is known to be more
effective—not to mention easier?

A MATTER OF PERCEPTION

Exercise scientists have tended to assume that *physiology* determines the intensity at which people naturally choose to exercise. Some researchers, for example, have proposed that most runners habitually run at intensities that fall slightly above the ventilatory threshold because they are either metabolically or biomechanically most efficient in that range. In fact, runners often are more efficient at their habitual pace, but this is simply because runners become more efficient at any pace they practice frequently. The evidence suggests that it is not physiology but *perception* that guides a recreational runner's initial selection of the pace that becomes habitual and eventually more efficient.

In 2001, researchers at Wayne State University asked a group of college volunteers to exercise for twenty minutes at a self-selected pace on each of three machines: a treadmill, a stationary bike, and a stair climber. Measurements of heart rate, oxygen consumption, and perceived effort were taken throughout all three workouts. The researchers expected to find that the subjects unconsciously targeted the same relative physiological intensity in each activity. Perhaps they would automatically exercise at 65 percent of their maximum heart rate regardless of which machine they were using. Or maybe they would instinctively settle into rhythm at 70 percent of their maximum rate of oxygen consumption in all three workouts. But that's not what happened. There was, in fact, no consistency in measurements of heart rate and oxygen consumption across the three disciplines. Instead, the subjects were found to have chosen the same level of perceived effort on the treadmill, the bike, and the stair climber.

The standard tool that scientists use to solicit ratings of perceived effort from participants in experiments like this one is the Borg Scale, which goes from 6 to 20 (don't ask why). On all three machines, the subjects in this study rated their effort at 12.5, which falls smack in the middle of the Borg Scale. An effort level of 13 on this scale is described as "somewhat hard." Although this level of perceived effort corresponds to disparate heart rates and oxygen-consumption levels in different activities, in all activities it corresponds to intensities that fall between the ventilatory threshold and the lactate threshold, or right where most recreational runners spend all too much of their training time.

One limitation of this study was that the subjects were not athletes. But other studies involving experienced runners have arrived at the same result. For example, in a 2012 study, researchers asked thirty female runners to run for thirty minutes on a treadmill at a self-selected pace. At the end of the run, the women were asked to rate their perceived effort on the Borg Scale. The average rating of perceived exertion (RPE) for the group was 12.79—just a tiny bit higher than it was among the nonathletes in the Wayne State study. What's more, the standard deviation from this average was a low 1.15, meaning all thirty women gave perceived effort ratings close to 12.79.

It may seem odd that runners do not naturally choose to train at an intensity that feels more comfortable. The reason, I believe, is that humans are naturally task oriented. When we have a job to do, we want to get it done. Of course, a twenty-minute workout is a twenty-minute workout, regardless of how fast you go. But humans evolved long before clocks existed, so we think in terms of covering distance rather than in terms of filling time even when we are on the clock.

Naturally, the fastest way to get a distance-based task such as a five-mile run over with is to treat it as a race and go all out. Maximal efforts come with a good deal of suffering, however, and humans have a natural aversion to suffering that is at least as powerful as our natural inclination to "get 'er done." So what do we do? We compromise between the desire to get the workout over with quickly and the desire not to suffer inordinately, and we end up doing the run (or the bike ride or the stair climb or whatever) at a moderate intensity.

INTENSITY BLINDNESS

Although an RPE of 12.5 (or 12.79) falls just below the number on the Borg Scale that corresponds to the description "somewhat hard," runners typically are not aware they are working somewhat hard when running at their habitual pace until they are asked to rate their effort. As a coach, I know that if I tell a runner to run a certain distance at an "easy" pace, it is very likely the runner will complete the run at her habitual pace, which is likely to fall in the moderate-intensity range. And if I ask the runner afterward if she ran easy as instructed, she will say that she did. In short, most runners think they are running easy (at low intensity) when in fact they are running "somewhat hard" (at moderate intensity).

This issue of *intensity blindness*, as I call it, was exposed in the ASU study I discussed earlier. What I did not share with you when I first described this study was that, before the researchers handed out heart rate monitors to their subjects, they asked the women to describe their own training in terms of intensity. On average, the runners claimed to do three low-intensity runs, one moderate-intensity run, and 1.5 high-intensity runs per week. This perception was far from reality. Whereas the runners believed they were doing three times more low-intensity running than moderate-intensity running, the heart rate data revealed they were in fact doing equal amounts of each.

If getting stuck in a rut of moderate intensity, as most runners do, resulted in inevitable catastrophe, it would not be so common. But this mistake rarely causes runners to go backward in their performance. More often, it merely reduces their rate of improvement, or, as in the case of Juan Carlos, it causes their progress to stall for a while. Because the progress-hindering effect of running too hard too often is typically less than catastrophic, most runners are not only unaware that their "easy" runs are not easy, but they are also unaware that the mistake is hurting them.

There's a song that says, "You only know you've been high when you're feeling low." Sometimes you need contrasting experience—something to compare your current situation against—before you realize things aren't the way they ought to be. In this respect, the problem of intensity blindness and its consequences among runners is not unlike the common issue of chronic low-grade sleep deprivation in the general population. If your optimal amount of sleep is eight hours per night and you routinely sleep seven hours, you may feel okay and be able to function fairly well during the day. It's only when something in your life changes (perhaps a new job with a shorter commute) that allows you to get an additional hour of sleep that you realize how much better you could have felt and functioned all along. Similarly, runners often need to experience what low-intensity running really feels like before they realize how hard they normally work when they run and how much it's been hindering their progress.

THE WEEK OF SLOW

As a coach, I keep runners from turning easy runs into "somewhat hard" runs by giving them specific pace, heart rate, and perceived-effort targets for each workout. Heart rate monitoring in particular is an effective tool for getting runners to slow down, while pace targets are better for getting runners to push themselves in the 20 percent of their workouts when they're supposed to. I will explain how to use heart rate, pace, and perceived effort to monitor and control the intensity of your runs in chapter 6. But before you start to use these guidelines, there is one challenge to take on right away—something I call *the week of slow*.

The week of slow is the running equivalent of a juice fast. Some people use short-term juice fasts to hit the reset button on their diet. The fast is not an end in itself. The goal is to make permanent changes to their diet, replacing bad habits with good ones. But instead of just making these changes from one day to the next, they first take a few days to break their attachments to the old habits by consuming nothing but healthy fruit and vegetable juices. Then, once they are no longer craving potato chips or whatever else, they return to a normal but improved diet.

The week of slow serves the same purpose for runners who wish to break out of the moderate-intensity rut. I came up with the practice spontaneously after I first learned about Stephen Seiler's 80/20 Rule. Although I was already doing all of my easy runs below the ventilatory threshold, I took a week to go even slower, and I learned that doing so helped me feel even better without sacrificing fitness. So I have been prescribing the practice to other runners ever since.

Here's how you do it: The next time you go for a run, go really slow. I mean, *really* slow. Don't pay attention to your heart rate or pace numbers. All of that comes later. It's perfectly okay if your pace on this run, and on all the runs in your week of slow, is even slower than you will be tasked to run on easy days in the 80/20 running program. You're not really in training yet. The point of the week of slow is to get you ready for 80/20 training by setting you free from your habitual pace and teaching you to embrace running slow. So just find a pace that feels completely comfortable, utterly free from strain. I don't care how much you have to slow down to reach this point—keep throttling back until you get there. If you're embarrassed to be seen running this slow on your usual trail, find another place to run where you won't be observed.

When you do this for the first time, the first thing you will realize when you find an effortless pace is that you were indeed straining a little at your habitual pace without being aware of it. This is an important revelation, and it constitutes the first step toward reaping the full benefits of 80/20 running. On the 80/20 program, you will never again feel this subtle strain during designated easy runs. Sure, some of these runs may last long enough to leave you feeling fatigued, but the *intensity* of your running should never again be the source of strain in your easy runs.

The next step, after you have locked onto this effortless feeling, is to keep your attention focused there. If you've ever tried Zen meditation—the kind during which you empty your mind—you know how hard it is to keep your thoughts from wandering for even ten seconds. Similarly, on the first day of your week of slow, your thoughts will wander, and when your thoughts wander, you will start to run faster, and when your attention eventually returns to your body, you will discover that you are running at your habitual pace and feeling the subtle strain you never really noticed before you forced yourself to slow down.

That's all right; it's part of the process. Just slow down again and get that effortless feeling back. Continue in this manner until you complete the run. Don't be surprised or discouraged if the run is a bit of a struggle. A tug-of-war will take place between your conscious efforts to enforce a slower pace and your instinctive urge to run at your habitual pace. Even though the slower pace will feel more comfortable, you won't get to fully enjoy it because of this internal struggle. Because the run promises to be mentally challenging in this way, it should be fairly short.

The next time you run, do the same thing but go a little farther. Find a slow pace that is so comfortable, you feel as though you could run forever. Every time you catch yourself speeding up, slow down again. You will probably find it somewhat easier to keep your pace slow in this second run, and you will more fully enjoy your freedom from the strain of your habitual pace.

TABLE 1.1   **3 SAMPLE "WEEK OF SLOW" SCHEDULES**

	LEVEL 1	LEVEL 2	LEVEL 3
DAY 1	2 miles	4 miles	5 miles
DAY 2		5 miles	6 miles
DAY 3	3 miles		7 miles
DAY 4		6 miles	
DAY 5	4 miles		8 miles
DAY 6		7 miles	9 miles
DAY 7	5 miles	8 miles	10 miles

Keep doing superslow runs of gradually increasing length until a full week has gone by. Table 1.1 presents three sample "week of slow" schedules for runners of different levels. Follow one of these or make up your own. By the time you get to the last run of the week, running very slowly will feel much more natural than it did on the first day. You will also enjoy running slow more because that feeling of total comfort won't be spoiled by a constant urge to push harder. You may also notice that you feel better generally: You aren't as tired at the end of each run, and you feel fresher at the start of the next. Some runners even get to the point where they look forward to their runs more and realize that running too hard was draining their motivation as well as hindering their progress. This is only a hint of the benefits that will come your way after you transition from the week of slow to regular 80/20 training.

Remember Juan Carlos, my client who was stuck at a 10K time of 52:30—and who, not coincidentally, was also stuck at a habitual training pace of 8:45 per mile, which for him was "somewhat hard"? After a week of slow and eleven weeks of 80/20 training, he lowered his 10K PR to 48:47. That's the power of slowing down.

THE EVOLUTION OF 80/20 RUNNING

The greatest runner of the nineteenth century was an English-man named Walter George. In 1886, George set a world re-cord of 4:12:75 for the mile that stood for twenty-nine years. Among the greatest runners today is Mo Farah, also an English-man (by way of Somalia). In 2013, Farah set a British record of 3:28.81 for 1500 meters, equivalent to 3:44 for the mile. That's almost half a minute, or 11 percent, faster than Walter George's mark.

Why are today's runners so much faster than those of the past? There's more than one reason. Much has changed in the sport over the past 150 years. In Walter George's time, only a handful of nations were serious about running, whereas today the sport is truly a global phenomenon. The talent pool has grown astro-nomically. There are technological differences as well. George raced on dirt and grass; Farah competes on advanced rubberized surfaces.

The biggest difference, however, is training. Early in his career, George ran no more than ten miles per week. Even when he set his long-standing mile record, he was averaging just three or four miles a day. Mo Farah started his career at seventy miles per week and moved up to 120 miles. This enormous difference in total running volume masks an even greater disparity in *low-intensity* running volume. Of the twenty-five miles Walter George ran in a typical week at his peak, sixteen were done at low intensity. Of the 120 miles Mo Farah runs in a typical week, close to one hundred are done below the ventilatory threshold. So, while Farah does just over 2.5 times more fast running than George did, he does six times more slow running.

If Walter George had been able to run on a rubberized track, and if he had enjoyed a higher level of competition, he certainly would have run the mile faster than 4:12—but not a whole lot faster. There's only so much you can achieve on less than four miles of running per day. Likewise, even with the advantages of modern competition and technology, Mo Farah would not have been able to run anywhere near the equivalent of a 3:44 mile on Walter George's training regimen. Differences in training methods clearly account for most of the improvement in race times that we have seen between the late nineteenth century and today.

Walter George's training methods were typical of his era, as are Mo Farah's of the present. The transition from the standard training system of the Victorian age—which featured small amounts of slow and fast running—to the modern training system—which is characterized by large quantities of slow running and modest doses of fast running—did not occur suddenly. It happened inch by inch, the way animals evolve.

In fact, the sport of running has much in common with evolution. Life on Earth is a game of survival of the fittest. So is running, in a slightly different sense. In life, genetically unique organisms compete to produce offspring. Genes that help an organism survive are likely to be passed on to future generations of the species, while genes that hinder survival tend to get weeded out. Over time, the species becomes increasingly adapted to its environment. In running, athletes build fitness with disparate methods and then come together to compete in races. The training methods used by race winners are frequently copied by the losers, who cast aside their own, inferior methods. Over time, this process generates an always improving set of best practices that in turn produces ever fitter and faster runners.

The two most important variables in run training are volume (how much you run) and intensity (how fast you run). These two variables have been combined in every conceivable way over the past 150 years. There have been low volume/low intensity runners, high volume/low intensity runners, low volume/high intensity runners, and high volume/high intensity runners. Each of these general approaches has encompassed a full range of permutations. The particular high volume/low intensity combination of one hundred to 120 miles of running per week and 80 percent of total running time at low intensity was first tried by elite runners in the 1950s. By the late 1960s, it had driven virtually every other way of combining volume and intensity into extinction, and it remains in almost universal use by today's elite runners.

In short, the 80/20 method has won the survival of the fittest, and there's nothing left to try. Let's see how it happened.

THE INTERVALS ERA

In July 1948, a successful Finnish businessman named Paavo Nurmi visited the Olympic training center in Uxbridge, England, a few days before the opening of the London Games. Nurmi was interested in watching the middle- and long-distance runners train. Among those whose workouts he witnessed was Emil Zátopek, a previously unheralded twenty-five-year-old Czech soldier who had recently come within two seconds of breaking the world record for 10,000 meters, which Nurmi himself had once held. He stared in astonishment as Zátopek ran five times 200 meters in 34 seconds, jogging briefly after each sprint, then ran 20 times 400 meters in times ranging from 56 to 75 seconds, again jogging between intervals, and finally ran another set of five 200 meter sprints. It was the hardest workout Nurmi had ever witnessed, and he had witnessed his share.

At the Olympics the following week Zátopek won a gold medal

in the 10,000 meters and took silver in the 5000. Upon returning to Finland, Nurmi urged the runners of his nation to emulate Zátopek's methods, declaring that "this athlete alone understood the meaning of hard training."

Here is a prime example of evolution at work in the sport of running. A young runner had come up with a novel training method that was different from what the established top runners of the day were doing. He then defeated those top runners in a major international competition. Afterward the losers were encouraged to copy the winner's methods, which would become the new standard until another young runner came up with something better still.

Paavo Nurmi probably wished he were twenty years younger and could put Zátopek's methods to use himself. At the peak of his career, Nurmi had run forty miles and walked twenty-five miles per week. This was more than the runners who came before him had done, and it was enough to make him the greatest runner in history. Known as the Flying Finn, Nurmi earned nine individual gold and silver medals in three Olympics between 1920 and 1928 and set numerous world records. Interestingly, Nurmi had been a rather mediocre runner until he added a relatively new method of training—high-intensity intervals—to his program. Workouts such as six times 400 meters in 60 seconds triggered a performance breakthrough that made the Flying Finn almost unbeatable for several years.

After he retired, though, Nurmi looked back on his career with regret, wishing he had done more interval work. "The greatest mistake I made, and which was formerly made in general, was the one-sided training program (too much long, slow running)," he told his biographer. He would live long enough (until 1973) to discover the error of this assessment.

If there is one thing Emil Zátopek did *not* do, it was "too much long, slow running." Zátopek was training much like the other young Czech runners of his generation—a few miles of easy jogging each day—when a buddy introduced him to the interval method in 1943. It was a eureka moment for him. "Why should I practice running slow?" he would later recall thinking. "I must learn to run fast by practicing to run fast."

Zátopek traded his five-mile jogs for a daily interval workout consisting of ten sprints of 100 or 200 meters plus six hard intervals of 400 meters. Plenty of other runners were doing intervals in those days, but Zátopek did *nothing but intervals*. And as time went by, he did more and more of them. His logic was simple: If a few intervals were good, more must be better.

Each year Zátopek increased his volume of interval training another step. The harder he trained, the faster he got. In 1949, he set a new world record of 29:02.6 for 10,000 meters. Two years later, he ran the fastest time in history for 20K. In 1952, he won four gold medals at the Olympics in Helsinki. Still not satisfied, he continued to ratchet up his training load.

By 1954, Zátopek was doing workouts that made the mind-blowing session Paavo Nurmi had witnessed at Uxbridge seem like a warm-up in comparison. He now ran *50 times 400 meters* at race intensity, and during peak training periods, he completed this heroic session two times a day every day. It added up to more than 140 miles per week, including recovery jogs, which accounted for only a third of the total volume. That year Zátopek set world records at 5000 meters (13:57.2) and again at 10,000 meters (28:54.2).

The next winter, Zátopek tried to raise his game another notch. In February, he ran as much as 180 miles in one week. But this time more intervals did not yield better performance. "I am no good this year," Zátopek, then thirty-three years old, announced after a series of lackluster results. He had exceeded the maximally effective dose of interval training. He had found his limit.

Zátopek could at least take consolation in knowing that his personal limit far surpassed that of any other living runner. As early as 1950, *Athletics Weekly* editor Jimmy Green had written, "Zátopek is, of course, a law unto himself when it comes to training, and no athlete would be wise to emulate his colossal amount of severe work. It combines the fast/slow/fast/slow work with punishing severity. The quantity and severity of his training and racing are such that it was fully anticipated he would not last for more than a couple of years at the same rate, but the Czech is still running and still breaking records."

Green was right about one thing: Zátopek was a law unto himself. Few of the runners who tried to match his murderous workload were able to, and perhaps only one runner—the Russian Vladimir Kuts—benefitted from it as much as Zátopek himself had. Half a decade younger than his idol, Kuts used high-volume interval training to win gold medals at 5000 and 10,000 meters at the 1956 Olympics and set world records at both distances. But his career was short. Zátopek's brutal regimen fried the legs off Kuts in less than five years.

Although his speed-based training system had taken the sport forward from where it had stood when Zátopek found it, that system proved to be a dead end. He had shown that high-intensity intervals were a vital ingredient in the training of distance runners, but in the final analysis, it seemed their place was rather smaller than Zátopek (and Nurmi) had anticipated. If future generations of runners were going to run even faster, they would have to do so by some means other than speed-based training.

MARATHONS FOR MILERS

When Emil Zátopek got the idea that lots of fast running was the key to maximum performance, he was working in a shoe factory in the city of Zlin, Czechoslovakia. Halfway around the world and a couple of years later, in 1945, in one of history's uncanny coincidences, Arthur Lydiard was working in a shoe factory in Auckland, New Zealand, when he came up with the idea that the key to maximum fitness was lots of *slow* running.

Lydiard was then twenty-seven years old, married, and a new

father. In his free time, he played club-level rugby and also jumped into the occasional track race for laughs, never running farther than a mile at a time in training. One day Lydiard was cajoled into running five miles—much farther than was his wont—by Jack Dolan, a central figure in the Auckland running community and a man on a mission to inspire young runners of promise to take the sport more seriously.

If Lydiard had performed well in this workout, it probably wouldn't have made a ripple in his life. But as it turned out, he got his ass kicked. Lydiard would later say that the run "nearly killed" him. This was an overstatement, but it's no exaggeration to say that Lydiard was thoroughly humiliated by the experience, for he took great pride in his fitness and he was quite a bit younger than Dolan. To have struggled so desperately to keep up with his middle-aged challenger in such a modest test of conditioning left a bitter taste in Lydiard's mouth, and he came away determined to erase it.

Another person in Lydiard's place might have added a bit more rigor to the fifteen-minute track workouts he did a couple of times a week. But intuition led Lydiard in another direction. As a rugby player, he was accustomed to sprinting, and he had good raw speed. Lack of speed was not the cause of his humiliation. The problem was stamina. In fact, Lydiard decided, lack of stamina was also the reason he lost even shorter contests, including the half-mile and one-mile track races in which he routinely got thumped by local studs like Norm Cooper and Bill Savidan. Lydiard had more than enough horsepower to beat those guys. What he did not have was the capacity to *sustain* his speed.

This problem was not unique to him. Lydiard realized that no runner truly needed to get faster in order to race faster over middle and long distances, because no runner, regardless of how gifted or how well trained he was, could sustain anything close to his maximum speed for even half a mile. But some runners could sustain a greater percentage of their natural speed over long distances than others could, and it was those runners—not necessarily the "fastest" runners—who won races. Endurance was the true limitation in running. And if that was the case, Lydiard concluded, then training should emphasize endurance building. The process of getting in shape for races should be a lopsided effort to increase stamina to the point where a runner could run more or less forever. *The secret to running faster was to run farther.*

Lydiard tested this idea first on himself. He started running every day. Once he was comfortable running every day, Lydiard bumped up the distance of his longest run to twelve miles. Before long, *all* of his runs were twelve miles. Still he did not feel tapped out, so he continued to pile on the miles, eventually maxing out at 250 miles in a single week. That was obviously too much. Two hundred miles per week wasn't much better. Ultimately, Lydiard discovered that he felt strongest when he ran one hundred to 120 miles per week and varied the distance of the individual workouts from day to day. A typical week, after he'd gotten it all figured out, looked something like this:

Monday: 10 miles
Tuesday: 15 miles
Wednesday: 12 miles
Thursday: 18 miles
Friday: 10 miles
Saturday: 15 miles
Sunday: 24 miles

Lydiard learned that no matter how tired he was from recent training, he could almost always manage to run again if he kept the pace slow. But he did not always run slowly. Lydiard played around with the intensity of his running almost as much as he did with the volume. These investigations taught him that speed work helped the most when it was sprinkled lightly on top of a huge foundation of slow running. In essence, he invented 80/20 training.

Although Lydiard raced sparingly during his *nine years* of experimentation, he raced better and better as he came closer and closer to perfecting his formula. He trained utterly alone through the better part of this period, but Lydiard's steadily improving results (which included national marathon championship titles in 1953 and 1955) and his boastful descriptions of the prodigious training distances that lay behind those results inspired other runners to join him.

His first regular training partner was Lawrie King, a young novice who worked alongside Lydiard at the shoe factory. In his first year of low-intensity, high-volume training, King struggled to a fifty-sixth place finish in the Auckland junior cross-country championship. A year later, he won the same race by seventy yards. A pattern was thus established that never changed: Lydiard's mostly-slow approach did not work overnight, but runners who stuck with it improved steadily year after year. King went on to win the senior New Zealand cross-country championship and even set a national record for six miles.

Almost before he knew it, Lydiard was surrounded by a half dozen young men on epic long runs through the Waitakere Ranges west of Auckland, and they were no longer his training buddies— he was their coach. Among those who sought Lydiard out were Murray Halberg, who started running after a rugby injury crippled his left arm; Barry Magee, a teenager who had just lost his father to an industrial accident; and Peter Snell, a big bruiser with a neck wider than his head. They didn't look like much, but on Lydiard's hundred-miles-per-week program, they began to win.

By the Olympic year of 1960, "Arthur's boys" were celebrated and feared throughout New Zealand. As a collective, they had won at least one national championship (usually more) each year since 1954. Five of them made the Olympic team. Halberg qualified for the Rome Games in both the 5000 meters and the 10,000 meters. Snell made the team at 800 meters. Magee claimed a spot in the marathon. A couple of second-tier athletes in Lydiard's group—Ray Puckett and Jeff Julian—took New Zealand's other two marathon slots.

In Rome, racing against runners conditioned on the currently dominant interval method, Arthur's boys won three medals—an unprecedented haul for the tiny country. Halberg took gold in the 5000. Snell also claimed gold and set an Olympic record in the 800. Magee snagged the bronze in the marathon.

Arthur's boys and their unconventional training methods were the story of the Rome Games. Evolution kicked in, and Lydiard's low-intensity, high-volume approach began to spread. Lydiard himself—an unabashed self-promoter—was the primary vehicle for the diffusion of his philosophy. In the spring of 1962 he wrote an article titled "Why I Prescribe Marathons for Milers" for *Sports Illustrated*.

"In theory," Lydiard explained, "I am trying to develop my runners until they are in a tireless state. In practice, this means I am trying to give them sufficient stamina to maintain their natural speed over whatever distance they are running. Stamina is the key to the whole thing, because you can take speed for granted. No? Look here. Everybody thinks a four-minute mile is terrific, but it is only four one-minute quarter miles. Practically any athlete can run a one-minute quarter, but few have the stamina to run four of them in a row. How do you give them the necessary stamina? By making them run and run and run some more."

Lydiard was in the United States when his *Sports Illustrated* article made its splash. He had been invited to tour the country for three months to deliver lectures at universities and anywhere else runners and coaches might gather. The first few events were standing room only, so the organizer extended the tour to eight months, during which time Lydiard's revolt became a revolution.

Over the next decade, a fascinating experiment was played out at the sport's highest level. Early adopters of the Lydiard system competed against speed-based training loyalists in all the big races, which became proxy battlefields where the two training systems struggled for dominance through their athletic avatars. Lydiard-style training finally won, but victory was not achieved overnight. At the 1964 Olympics in Tokyo, the men's 800 meters and 1500 meters were won by Peter Snell, one of Arthur's boys; the men's 5000 meters was won by American Bob Schul, who practiced speed-based training; and the men's 10,000 meters was won by another American, Billy Mills, then a recent convert to the Lydiard system.

Mills was an interesting case. He never won an individual NCAA title while running thirty miles per week for the University of Kansas. After graduating, Mills relocated to Houston, where he came under the influence of Pat Clohessy, an Australian runner and one of Lydiard's earliest disciples. In the lead-up to his stunning breakthrough at the Tokyo Games, Mills ran up to ninety mostly slow miles per week.

Such stories inspired yet more runners to take a chance on the Lydiard system. By 1972, it was impossible for a runner with any amount of natural talent to win on the world stage with speed-based training. At the Olympic Games in Munich, the winners of the men's 800 meters (American Dave Wottle), 1500 meters (Finland's Pekka Vasala), 5000 meters (Finland's Lasse Viren), and 10,000 meters (Viren again) were all adherents of the low-intensity, high-volume way. But even then the Lydiard system had only begun to prove its might.

THE BOSTON RENAISSANCE

During his 1962 tour of the United States, Arthur Lydiard made a brief stop in Des Moines, Iowa. Among those who attended Lydiard's lecture there was Bill Squires, a former All-American miler at Notre Dame who had just started coaching high school runners in Boston. He became an instant convert. When Squires returned to Boston, he brought Lydiard's ideas with him.

Eleven years later, Squires became the head coach of the newly created Greater Boston Track Club. Having gotten good results from Lydiard-style training with younger runners, he applied the same mostly-slow approach with the adult members of the GBTC, many of whom had cut their teeth on speed-based training. The outcome was immediate success, which attracted new talent to the club, which resulted in even greater success, attracting still more talent.

One of the first runners to join up was a twenty-five-year-old hospital janitor named Bill Rodgers. Eighteen months later, Rodgers won the Boston Marathon with an American record time of 2:09:55. Under Squires' guidance, "Boston Billy" went on to claim three more Boston Marathon victories, lowering his American record to 2:09:27 in the 1979 race. He won the New York City Marathon four times as well.

Table 2.1 offers a seven-day sample of Bill Rodgers' training from two weeks before his first win in Boston. He ran 128 miles in those seven days. It is impossible to accurately judge intensity from the information Rodgers recorded, but my best guess is that the distances emphasized in boldface were run at or above the ventilatory threshold. If so, then Rodgers completed 104 of his 128 miles for the week—or 81 percent—at low intensity. He did not know it, but he was following the 80/20 Rule.

In 1976 a talented local high school runner named Alberto Salazar joined the GBTC. Three years later, at age nineteen, Salazar won the U.S. national cross-country championship. The second-, fourth-, and fifth-place finishers in that race were also GBTC members. By that time Salazar had left Boston to become a student at the University of Oregon, where he was coached by Bill Dellinger, one of the first apostles of the Lydiard system, having visited New Zealand to learn from the master in 1962. After graduating from Oregon, Salazar set American records for 5000 meters (13:11.93), 10,000 meters (27:25.61), and the marathon (lowering Rodgers' mark to 2:08:13).

Another early member of the GBTC was Bob Sevene, who had previously used speed-based training as a member of the Army Elite team before switching to low-intensity, high-volume training under Bill Squires and discovering a whole new dimension of fitness. In 1983, Sevene became the coach of Joan Benoit, still a raw talent at age twenty-six, and taught her the same mostly-slow training method that Squires had taught him and that Lydiard

TABLE 2.1 BILL RODGERS' TRAINING, APRIL 7–13, 1975

MONDAY	7 miles @ noon—flat, good pace 12 miles @ 3:30 pm—slow, easy hills 19 total
TUESDAY	7+ miles @ noon—okay pace, flat 10+ miles—**12 x 1/2 @ 2:28, 2 x 1m @ 4:51, 4:56—3 min jog between, 2 down** 18 total
WEDNESDAY	8 miles @ noon—good pace, flat 12+ miles—good pace, flat 20+ total
THURSDAY	18 miles @ 4:15 pm—okay pace, some easy hills
FRIDAY	7+ miles @ 1 pm—flat 3 miles @ 6:15 pm **4 x 1m @ 4:49 w/480 yd jog** [length of BC track] 3 miles after 18+ total
SATURDAY	8 miles @ 10:30 am—easy, flat, pit stops? **12 miles @ 5 pm—hard pace,** flat 20 total
SUNDAY	15 miles @ 11:30 am—fairly hilly
TOTAL MILES: MILES AT LOW INTENSITY:	128 104 (81%)

had taught Squires. On the strength of this method, Benoit won three Boston Marathon titles and the first Olympic Women's Marathon. She also set American records in the half marathon and marathon and a world record at the latter distance.

Perhaps the best proof of the potency of Lydiard's de facto 80/20 running system as it was applied within the Greater Boston Track Club was what it did for many runners of less talent than Rodgers, Salazar, and Benoit. Take Dick Mahoney. Mahoney was working full-time as a mailman when he finished the 1979 Boston Marathon in 2:14:36. That time was good enough for tenth place, but it only got him fourth place among GBTC members, behind Rodgers (the winner), Bob Hodge (third in 2:12:30), and Tom Fleming (fourth in 2:12:56).

The GBTC fell back to earth in the early 1980s, when the sport became professionalized and the top runners were siphoned off by shoe companies. But by then the low-intensity, high-volume training system that made the GBTC the most dominant running club the world has ever seen had spread across the country. No new method has come along since then to surpass the mostly-slow approach.

A survey of male and female runners who competed in the 2004 U.S. Olympic Team Trials Men's and Women's Marathons revealed that the men did almost three-quarters of their training slower than their marathon race pace, while the women did more than two-thirds of their training at slower paces. At the elite level, marathon pace is just a notch above the ventilatory threshold, so the athletes involved in this survey were not far away from unconscious obedience to the 80/20 Rule.

THE RISE OF KENYA

In 1983, a Greater Boston Track Club member, Greg Meyer, won the Boston Marathon for the last time. Five years later, a Kenyan male won the event for the first time. Ibrahim Hussein's victory marked the dawn of the Kenyan dynasty in distance running. Incredibly, Kenyan men have won all but seven runnings of the Boston Marathon since '88.

Kenya's rise to supremacy in international running is looked back on as a story of overnight success that was made possible almost entirely by the Kenyan people's natural gift for running. But this view is not accurate. The first Kenyan runners to race internationally got spanked. In 1954, a pair of Kenyan runners took part in a London track meet. Nyandika Maiyoro finished a distant third in a three-mile race and Lazara Chepkwony failed to complete the six-mile event. At the Melbourne Olympics two years later, Maiyoro took seventh at 5000 meters, Arere Anentia failed to qualify for the 1500-meter final, and Arap Sum Kanuti finished thirty-first in the marathon. Kanuti was still the best athlete his country could muster for the Rome games four years later, where he slid back to fifty-ninth place in the marathon.

Kenyan runners would never have become the leading force in running that they are today if not for a fortuitous accident. British missionaries in Kenya endeavored to spread both Christianity and education there by building schools such as St. Patrick's High School in Iten, which opened its doors in 1961. Many of the children who attended these schools ran to and from class daily, motorized transportation being a luxury few could afford. The missionaries certainly had no intention of putting thousands of Kenyan boys and girls on a low-intensity, high-volume running program, but that's essentially what happened.

When Arthur Lydiard visited Kenya for the first time in 1992, he was blown away by how much running the children there did for transportation. It was exactly what he would have required the children of his own country to do if he were charged with making New Zealand the most powerful running nation on earth. At the time of Lydiard's visit to Kenya, high-intensity interval training was enjoying a second life in the American high school system. Lydiard, of course, was horrified. After returning home, he wrote a letter to the magazine *American Track & Field*, in which he begged America's coaches to take a cue from East Africa.

"When Swedish physiologists went to observe and analyze the training methods of the Kenyan runners," Lydiard wrote, "they found that high school girls and boys were running on average about twelve or thirteen miles daily to and from school. Whereas the Africans would be running leisurely, trotting to and from school, their counterparts in the U.S. would be mostly on the track doing hard anaerobic repetitions. This is where the real problem lies."

Jogging to school, though, was not enough to establish Kenya as a global powerhouse in the sport of running. It was also necessary that college-age and adult Kenyans start to use Lydiard-style training to prepare for elite competition. This didn't happen until the mid-1970s, when coaches at American universities initiated the practice of offering scholarships to gifted young Kenyan athletes. The first generation of Kenyan sporting émigrés included

Henry Rono, who enrolled at Washington State University in 1976. After two years of low-intensity, high-volume training, Rono broke four world records in a span of eighty-one days.

Lydiard-style training came to Kenya at about the same time. While Henry Rono was breaking records in Europe, an Irish missionary named Colm O'Connell took over the running program at St. Patrick's High School. O'Connell had zero background as a running coach, but he boned up on the sport and wisely settled on a mostly-slow approach with his young athletes. One of his first protégés was the above-mentioned Ibrahim Hussein, whose marathon training closely resembled that of Bill Rodgers a decade before.

There is a popular belief that Kenyan runners do much more training at moderate and high intensities than do elite runners from other places, but the hard data does not support this myth. In 2003, top French exercise scientist Veronique Billat collected training data from twenty elite male and female Kenyan runners. A subsequent analysis of the data conducted by Stephen Seiler revealed that these runners did 85 percent of their running below the lactate threshold. Since the lactate threshold is slightly higher than the ventilatory threshold, these runners probably did very close to 80 percent of their training below the latter.

Toby Tanser's book *More Fire* is a treasure trove of information about Kenyan training methods. Table 2.2 is borrowed from its pages. The table presents a sample week of training for Lornah Kiplagat, a legendary Kenyan runner who set a half-marathon world record of 1:06:25 in 2007. I've taken the liberty of adding emphasis to the words "easy," "recovery," and "warm-up" to draw attention to just how large a fraction of her total mileage was run at low intensity. If we make the reasonable assumption that the efforts described with these terms fell below the ventilatory threshold, then like the American marathoners mentioned above, Kiplagat did about 80 percent of her training at low intensity, as all elite runners today do, Kenyans included.

TABLE 2.2   A TYPICAL WEEK OF TRAINING FOR AN
ELITE KENYAN RUNNER

	MORNING	AFTERNOON
MONDAY	45 min. **recovery run**	45 min. **recovery** run
TUESDAY	45 min. **easy**	20 min. **warm-up** 3 x 400m (1 min. **recovery**), 800m (2 min. **recovery**), 1200 (3 min. **recovery**), 1600m
WEDNESDAY	45 min. **recovery**	60 min. **recovery**
THURSDAY	60 min. **easy**	1 hr. 20 min. hill work, running in sand dunes
FRIDAY	45 min. **recovery**	60 min. **recovery**
SATURDAY	60 min. **easy**	45 min. medium
SUNDAY	Long run, 2 hrs. 10 min. Break-up: 20 min. **easy**, 30 min. medium, 20 min. fast, 20 min. **easy**, 20 min. fast and 20 min. **easy**	

In 2011, the BBC sent former miler Eamonn Coghlan to Kenya in search of the secret to their running dominance. In the first episode of the three-part documentary, he met with Colm O'Connell at St. Patrick's High School, where they watched a group of O'Connell's runners running slowly in single-file formation around and around a grass soccer field.

"Is this still part of their warm-up?" Coghlan asked.

"This is the workout," O'Connell said.

"And they won't go any harder?" Coghlan asked.

"This is it," O'Connell said.

FROM MOSTLY SLOW TO 80/20

Training methods continue to evolve in the sport of running, but today's innovators are working at the margins, tinkering with

different methods of incorporating cross-training, altitude training, and other such practices into their regimens. The bigger
questions of how much and how fast to run appear to have been
answered once and for all. With respect to these two key variables, Mo Farah's training in the second decade of the twenty-
first century is not much different from Bill Rodgers' training in
the 1970s. Rodgers ran upward of 120 miles per week, and Farah
runs up to that amount. Rodgers did about 80 percent of his running at low intensity, and Farah does the same.

Yet while both knew their training distances, neither realized he
was following the 80/20 Rule. Runners routinely measure and track
their volume, but they do not monitor their intensity distribution in
the rigorous manner that scientists have begun to do. Every runner
knows how many miles she ran last week, but does any runner know
what percentage of his total running time for the past week was
spent at heart rates below his individual ventilatory threshold?

Because intensity distribution is not normally measured and
tracked, elite runners like Mo Farah, who are clearly balancing the
intensity of their training optimally, don't actually realize what they
are doing quantitatively. They do, of course, consciously manipulate intensity in their training, but they tend to do so in terms of
workout frequency (typically executing ten slow runs and two or
three faster runs per week) rather than in terms of time spent in
each intensity zone. Only very recently have scientists analyzed the
training data of elite runners and discovered that nearly all of them
follow the 80/20 Rule. That they do so without conscious awareness
is a powerful indication that 80/20 running is truly optimal, because that's how evolution works—solving problems blindly.

This kind of evidence does not satisfy most scientists, though.
They want to see proof from traditional, controlled studies that
the 80/20 Rule works better than other ways of balancing intensities in training. This proof now exists, and it's piling up quickly.
Most important, this new research proves that the 80/20 Rule
works not just for elite runners but also for everyday runners like
you and me.

3.

THE 80/20 BREAKTHROUGH

Though Stephen Seiler's discovery of the 80/20 Rule was somewhat accidental, it appears to be an innovation that he was born to make. Seiler grew up in Texas and Arkansas in the 1970s, developing a passion for science at an age when most boys are more interested in video games. His mother granted him permission to set up a "laboratory" underneath a staircase in the family home. There he played around with a microscope, test tubes, and other such instruments every day after school.

Seiler liked sports too—particularly football and track and field—but he viewed these interests as entirely separate from his scientific endeavors until a fateful day when, at the age of fifteen, he came across a copy of *Jim Fixx's Second Book of Running*. It contained a chapter called "The Scientists of Sport." Seiler read it and knew immediately what he was going to do professionally when he grew up.

Seiler pursued a bachelor's degree in exercise science at the University of Arkansas and subsequently stayed on to earn his master's degree. During this time, he took up competitive cycling and got pretty good at it, winning some local races.

In 1989, Seiler entered a PhD program at the University of Texas. While he was in Austin, he gave up cycling in favor of rowing, which he was *really* good at—good enough to win a handful of masters national championships in various boat classes. When

Seiler was close to completing his dissertation on heart attacks in mice, he attended a meeting of the American College of Sports Medicine, where he met and fell in love with a Norwegian woman.

Soon married, Seiler moved to Norway and resumed his research at Agder University in the city of Kristiansand. The most popular endurance sport in Norway is cross-country skiing. Seiler became interested in the way high-level Nordic skiers trained, especially when he observed Olympic-caliber athletes sometimes *walking* up steep hills to keep their heart rate from creeping above the low-intensity zone. "They had what I came to call excellent intensity discipline," Seiler told me.

He decided to formally study the training of these athletes, as well as that of elite rowers. Seiler developed a plan to use painstaking data collection and analysis to determine exactly how much of their total training time was spent at various intensities—something that had never been done before. What he ultimately discovered would surprise him and many others.

HOW DO THE BEST ENDURANCE ATHLETES REALLY TRAIN?

In one of his early studies, Seiler collected and analyzed data on the training of twelve elite junior cross-country skiers. He found that 75 percent of their workouts were devoted entirely to low-intensity training. When Seiler mixed all of the workouts together and looked at the actual time spent at each level of intensity, he saw that 91 percent of their total training time was spent below the ventilatory threshold. In other words, the skiers devoted slightly less than 80 percent of their workouts to low-intensity work and spent a little more than 80 percent of their total training time at low intensity.

In another early study, Seiler investigated historical trends in the training of elite Norwegian rowers. He tracked changes in training patterns between 1970 and 2001 and found that between these dates, the amount of low-intensity training that the country's top rowers did increased by 67 percent, while the amount of training they performed at moderate and high intensities decreased by almost 60 percent. Within the same thirty-two-year time span, the performance level of the best Norwegian rowers (as measured by a standard six-minute time trial) increased by 10 percent. By 2001, Norway's elite rowers were doing an average of fifty hours of low-intensity training and seven hours of moderate- and high-intensity training per month. That works out to a ratio of 88/12.

Seiler couldn't help but wonder if the same pattern of mostly-slow training was present in other endurance sports. He looked around for existing studies by other researchers and found that it was.

In 1995, a team of French researchers tracked the distribution of training intensities in a group of elite swimmers over the course of an entire season. They found that these athletes did 77 percent of their training at low intensity and 23 percent at moderate and high intensities.

In 2007, Augusto Zapico and colleagues at the University of Madrid tracked the training of Spanish cyclists on an elite under-twenty-three team during two four-month periods. In the first period, they did 78 percent of their training at low intensity and improved significantly in performance tests. In the second period, they did only 70 percent of their training at low intensity and did not improve at all.

In 2012, Iñigo Mujika of the University of Basque Country monitored the training of elite triathlete Ainhoa Murua as she prepared for the London Olympics (where she placed seventh). Over a period of fifty weeks, she did 74 percent of her swimming, 88 percent of her cycling, 85 percent of her running, and 83 percent of her combined training below the lactate threshold (which, remember, is slightly above the ventilatory threshold).

And runners? In 2001, Veronique Billat collected training data from elite male and female marathon runners from France and Portugal. She found that they did 78 percent of their training at speeds slower than their marathon race speed, which, as I've already noted, falls one notch above the ventilatory threshold for elite men runners. In the previous chapter, I mentioned a pair of studies, one also done by Billat, which produced similar results.

When it was all said and done, Stephen Seiler had discovered that elite athletes in *all* endurance sports do approximately 80 percent of their training at low intensity. In some sports, this 80/20 Rule applies on a session basis. For example, cross-country skiers devote roughly one in five (or 20 percent) of their workouts to high-intensity training, but they spend somewhat less than 20 percent of their total training time at high intensity because their slower workouts tend to last longer. In other sports, including running, the 80/20 Rule applies on a time basis. Top runners everywhere spend close to eight out of every ten minutes of training time at low intensity. Despite these slightly different applications of the 80/20 Rule, the similarity of training intensity distributions across endurance sports is uncanny, especially when you consider that each sport evolved independently of the rest.

As a runner, you might be wondering why you should care that athletes in other endurance sports balance the intensity of their training the same way runners do. The existence of this pattern in a variety of sports provides strong further evidence that the evolution of the 80/20 phenomenon in running was not arbitrary but instead came about as the optimal solution to the problem of maximizing human running performance.

Cycling, swimming, triathlon, and other endurance sports are close cousins of running. Although there are obvious surface differences (swimming is upper-body dominant, cycling is nonimpact, and so forth), at their core, all endurance disciplines are the same. Success in each of them depends on the ability to sustain aggressive submaximal speeds over long distances. The type of fitness that supports sustained speed in one endurance discipline differs only marginally from the type of fitness that does so in any other discipline. Therefore the training methods that generate maximal fitness must also be similar across all endurance disciplines. The chances that athletes in all endurance sports would converge on the same 80/20 formula by sheer coincidence after starting in different places are next to zero. This could only have happened because the 80/20 formula works better than any alternative in each sport.

80/20 AND THE EVERYDAY RUNNER

When Stephen Seiler began to lecture on the 80/20 Rule in the early 2000s, he got a lot of pushback from his fellow exercise scientists. He wasn't too surprised. Exercise scientists have long been enamored with high-intensity interval training, and indeed there is plenty of research which seems to suggest that "HIIT" is more effective than low-intensity training.

I'll give you one example. In 2008, researchers at Old Dominion University gathered sixty-one "healthy young adults" (translation: college students) and divided them into four groups. For six weeks, members of one group did high-intensity workouts on a stationary bike three times per week. Members of a second group trained more often (four times per week) but at a lower intensity (moderate). The third group also trained four times per week but their workouts lasted 50 percent longer and were done at low intensity. The fourth group did not exercise.

Before and after the six-week training period, all of the subjects completed a VO_2max test, which measures aerobic capacity, or the capacity to use oxygen to support muscle work. Despite spending 30 percent less time exercising, members of the high-intensity group experienced an almost twofold greater improvement in VO_2max than did members of the low-intensity group.

In a 2012 review of existing research on the question of high intensity versus low intensity, McMaster University's Martin Gibala concluded, "A growing body of evidence demonstrates that high-intensity interval training (HIIT) can serve as an effective alternate [sic] to traditional endurance-based training, inducing similar or even superior physiological adaptations in

healthy individuals and diseased populations, at least when compared on a matched-work basis."

This conclusion is true as far as it goes, but it does not support
the notion that a speed-based training approach is better for runners and other endurance athletes than a mostly-slow approach.
The reason, as Stephen Seiler well knew, is that the studies upon
which it is based are far removed from the real world. For starters, the subjects are always nonathletes, never trained runners.
How would the results of the Old Dominion study have differed
if the subjects had come into the experiment having already developed their aerobic capacity with prior training? Another thing
to consider is that a VO_2max test is not a running race. As we will
see in the next chapter, running fitness encompasses more than
just aerobic capacity.

These are small matters. A much bigger issue is time scale. The
Old Dominion study I just described lasted six weeks. Runners
typically take far more time to build peak fitness for races. Fur-
thermore, the subjects of this study did the same workouts
throughout the six-week intervention. That's not like the real
world, where runners increase their overall workload bit by bit.
Nor was the rigid segregation of training types like the real
world, where most runners who take a speed-based approach do
some low-intensity workouts and runners who practice Lydiard-
style training do *some* high-intensity workouts. But in the studies
it's all or nothing.

Seiler felt that his analysis of the training of world-class athletes offered better evidence in favor of 80/20 training for endurance athletes than experiments like the Old Dominion study
offered against it. But he recognized that in order to win over the
skeptics he needed even better evidence. Specifically, he needed
controlled studies where real athletes training for real races were
placed on either an 80/20 program or a speed-based program
and the results were compared. No sooner had he acknowledged
this need than the opportunity to fulfill it came from a Spaniard
named Jonathan Esteve-Lanao.

Like Seiler, Esteve-Lanao is an exercise scientist, but he is also a running coach and a runner. He's a very good runner too, with personal best times of 3:54 for 1500 meters and 1:11:30 for the half marathon. He coaches a large running club in Madrid and teaches at the European University of Madrid. In 2003, Esteve-Lanao posed the same question Stephen Seiler had been exploring in Norway: How do endurance athletes really train? But Esteve-Lanao chose a different way to address this question. Instead of simply calculating the average distribution of training intensities in a group of athletes, he wanted to look at individual differences and find out whether runners who did more slow running performed better in races.

Esteve-Lanao recruited eight members of his running club to participate in a study. They were all young (twenty-one to twenty-five years), male, and fast, with an average 5K time of 15:22. He gave out heart rate monitors to the runners and demanded that the devices be worn during every run for twenty-four weeks as the runners prepared for the Spanish national cross-country championship, a race of just over ten kilometers. After the race, Esteve-Lanao calculated how much time each runner had spent in each of three intensity zones. "Low intensity" was defined as the range of heart rates that fell below the ventilatory threshold. "High intensity" was specified as the range of heart rates falling above another threshold called the respiratory compensation point, where hyperventilation begins. This threshold is a little higher than the lactate threshold, and it occurred at 91 percent of maximum heart rate for these subjects, which is typical for trained runners. The space between these two thresholds was defined as "moderate intensity."

On average, the runners spent 71 percent of their total training time at low intensity, 21 percent at moderate intensity, and 8 percent at high intensity during their twenty-four weeks of training. The numbers were not the same for all of the runners, however. Some runners spent more than 71 percent of their total time at low intensity, others less, and the differences were strongly predictive of differences in race performance. The individual runner who spent the most time at low intensity during training recorded the fastest time on race day, while the runner who spent the least time at low intensity produced the slowest race time. Fitness tests conducted periodically throughout the study period showed that all of the runners became significantly fitter, but those who spent closer to 80 percent of their total training time at low intensity improved the most.

Intrigued by these results, which were published in 2005, Esteve-Lanao decided to conduct a follow-up study to determine whether this correlation was merely coincidental or was actually causal. At this same time, he learned about the work of Stephen Seiler and his 80/20 Rule. Esteve-Lanao contacted Seiler and asked if he would be willing to help him conduct the follow-up study. Seiler leaped at the opportunity.

In this second experiment, Esteve-Lanao and Seiler chose not merely to observe the training of real runners but to actively manipulate it. Again, Esteve-Lanao recruited subjects from his club. He ended up with twelve young men (ages twenty-five to twenty-nine) with 10K times ranging from 30 to 35 minutes. Six of the runners were placed on a training program that *required* them to do 80 percent of their running at low intensity and the other 20 percent at moderate to high intensity for five months. The remaining six runners were instructed to do just 65 percent of their training at low intensity and the rest at moderate and high intensities. Total training distance was held equal between the two groups, at an average of 50 to 55 miles per week.

Before the five-month training period began, all twelve subjects completed a 10.4-kilometer simulated cross-country race. At the end of the training period, the same race was repeated. The point of the experiment, of course, was to determine which training program produced the biggest improvement in performance. In the initial test, members of the 65/35 group achieved an average time of 37:51. Five months later, their average time for the same distance dropped down to 35:50. That's an improvement of

2:01, or 5.3 percent. Members of the 80/20 group, meanwhile, achieved an average time of 37:29 in the first simulated cross-country race and a time of 34:52 in the second. That's an improvement of 2:37, or 7 percent. The difference between a 2:01 improvement in race time and a 2:37 improvement is 30 percent, which is massive by the standards of competitive runners.

Esteve-Lanao and Seiler presented their results in a paper published in the *Journal of Strength and Conditioning Research* in 2007. They concluded, "The present data suggest that if the runner can dedicate more time to daily training sessions, it seems better to design an 'easy-hard' distribution of load (increasing the amount of low-intensity training) than a 'moderately hard–hard' approach."

This left Esteve-Lanao wondering: What if a runner can't or doesn't want to dedicate more time to training? While the subjects of his second study did not run anywhere near as much as elite runners do, their average weekly volume of fifty to fifty-five miles was still greater than the average runner's training volume. Many runners in the recreationally competitive category believe that by running faster in training, they can compensate for running less. They figure that running thirty miles per week mostly at moderate to high intensity will make them just as fit as running sixty miles mostly at low intensity. Esteve-Lanao and Seiler rather doubted it. They wanted to find out if an 80/20 training-intensity balance was also optimal for recreational runners who ran less than the more competitive members of Esteve-Lanao's running club, so they teamed up once again to design a study.

Esteve-Lanao went back to his club for subjects, this time choosing thirty runners with average 10K times of just under 40 minutes—better than average but far from elite. As in the previous study, the subjects were divided into two groups. Members of one group were asked to do 80 percent of their training below the ventilatory threshold and the remaining 20 percent above it. Members of the second group were asked to do 50 percent of their training at low intensity and most of the remaining 50 percent at moderate intensity (between the ventilatory and respiratory compensation thresholds). As I mentioned in chapter 1, research has demon-strated that the average recreationally competitive runner main-tains an approximate 50/50 intensity balance in her training. The study was essentially set up to compare the 80/20 approach against the typical training approach of runners in this category.

All thirty runners were given heart rate monitors and told to wear them during every run for ten weeks. Members of both groups ran an average of 30 to 40 miles per week, a training vol-ume that is attainable (if not immediately, then eventually) by most recreationally competitive runners. Subjects in the 50/50 group spent slightly less time running than did those in the 80/20 group so that the training *load* (which factors in both vol-ume and intensity) was equal for the two groups. But because those in the 50/50 group did more running at higher speeds, they covered the same distance as the 80/20 group. Before the training period began, all of the subjects completed a 10K time trial to establish a performance baseline. This test was repeated at the end of the training period to measure progress.

When the ten weeks were up, Esteve-Lanao noticed a problem with the data. Most members of the 80/20 group had not done as they were told. Each of them had spent too much time at moderate intensity (which Esteve-Lanao and Seiler refer to as zone 2) and too little at low intensity (zone 1). Esteve-Lanao suspected that the fault lay with his allowing the runners to train with fellow club members.

"When they run in groups," he told me, "sometimes some of them go at a little higher intensity than the prescribed one." Any runner who has experienced group training is familiar with this effect. The strongest runner sets the pace, and the others follow like lemmings.

The experiment was not quite ruined, however. On average, members of the 80/20 group had spent 72.9 percent of their total training time at low intensity while members of the 50/50 group had done 46.8 percent of their running below the ventilatory threshold. So there was still a basis for comparison.

As it turned out, the runners who did about half of their training at low intensity lowered their 10K time from an average of 39:24 to 38:00. That's an improvement of 1:24, or 3.5 percent. Those who did roughly 73 percent of their training at low intensity lowered their 10K time from an average of 39:18 to 37:19. That's an improvement of 1:59, or 5.0 percent.

Most runners, if offered a choice between a training program that promised to lower their 10K time by 1:24 and another program that promised to lower their 10K time by 1:59, would choose the latter in a heartbeat—especially if they knew the more effective program was also easier.

What's more, the margin of improvement was even greater among six members of the 80/20 group who had adhered most faithfully to the instructions, completing an average of 78 percent of their training at low intensity. These runners had lowered their 10K times by an average of 7 percent, which was statistically significant compared to the 50/50 group.

Overall, the results of this study strengthened Esteve-Lanao and Seiler's hunch that 80/20 training was more effective for all runners, including low-mileage recreationally competitive runners. But they came away from it feeling that the case for the 80/20 approach was not yet complete.

THE SALZBURG STUDY

One of the great things about science is that it is collaborative in the broadest sense. When an individual scientist or a team of scientists begins to publish intriguing new research on a particular question, it is common for other scientists to step forward and add their own contributions. That's a blessing, because experiments like those that Jonathan Esteve-Lanao and Stephen Seiler have done together take a long time to plan and execute. Seven years passed between the publication of their first coauthored paper and their second, which appeared in 2014. If it was up to them alone to see this line of research through to a final conclusion, it would take a lifetime. Fortunately, other scientists have lately taken an interest in Esteve-Lanao and Seiler's work and have begun to make their own contributions.

Among these other scientists are Thomas Stöggl of the University of Salzburg, Austria, and Billy Sperlich of Mid Sweden University. Stöggl and Sperlich are not interested in the 80/20 intensity balance itself so much as they are interested in a concept called *polarized training*. The 80/20 method and polarized training are closely related but differ slightly in their emphasis. The emphasis in 80/20 training is placed on maximizing low-intensity training. What's important is ensuring that a full 80 percent of total training time is spent at low intensity. Exactly how the remaining 20 percent of training time is divided between moderate intensity and high intensity is less important.

In polarized training, the emphasis is placed on *minimizing moderate-intensity training*. Advocates of polarized training believe that the greatest mistake in endurance training is spending too much time at moderate intensity, which is more stressful than low intensity yet less beneficial than high intensity. Like the champions of 80/20 training, they argue that low-intensity work should account for most of an athlete's total training time, but they are less concerned about hitting the 80 percent mark.

A training program can be both 80/20 and polarized, and in fact the lower-intensity training program used in Esteve-Lanao and Seiler's 2014 study was just that. The runners in the 80/20 group were asked to do 80 percent of their training at low intensity, 20 percent at high-intensity, and *none* at moderate intensity. It was this polarized aspect that Stöggl and Sperlich picked up on and decided to test in their own study.

The key advantage of the Salzburg study in relation to previous studies was its scope. Its subjects were forty-eight athletes representing four sports: running, cross-country skiing, cycling, and triathlon. Runners made up the largest block, with twenty-one subjects. The scope of the Salzburg study was also greater with respect to the comparisons it made. Instead of testing only two training protocols, Stöggl and Sperlich compared four. Twelve athletes, representing a mix of sports, were assigned to each group. All four groups trained for nine weeks, but each was assigned its own combination of volume and intensity.

The "high-volume" group did 83 percent of their training at low intensity, 16 percent at moderate intensity, and 1 percent at high intensity. The "threshold" group did 46 percent of their training at low intensity, 54 percent at moderate intensity, and 0 percent at high intensity. The "high-intensity" group did 43 percent of their training at low intensity, 0 percent at moderate intensity, and 57 percent at high intensity. Finally, the "polarized" group did 68 percent of their training at low intensity, 6 percent at moderate intensity, and 26 percent at high intensity. The more training a given group did at moderate and/or high intensity, the less total training it did, such that training loads were roughly equal.

Before the nine-week training period began, all of the athletes completed a performance test. For the runners, this test consisted of an incremental running test to exhaustion. The treadmill was started at a very low speed of 4.5 mph. The speed was then increased by just over 1 mph every 30 seconds until the athlete couldn't continue. Stöggl and Sperlich noted how long each runner lasted and also the top speed he reached before quitting. The same tests were repeated at the conclusion of the nine-week training period.

TABLE 3.1   A SUMMARY OF THE SALZBURG STUDY

	% TRAINING AT LOW INTENSITY	% TRAINING AT MODERATE INTENSITY	% TRAINING AT HIGH INTENSITY	CHANGE IN TIME TO EXHAUSTION	CHANGE IN PEAK SPEED/POWER
HIGH-VOLUME GROUP	83	16	1	+8.0%	−1.5%
THRESHOLD GROUP	46	54	0	+6.2%	+1.8%
HIGH-INTENSITY GROUP	43	0	57	+8.8%	+4.4%
POLARIZED GROUP	68	6	24	+17.4%	+5.1%

The biggest performance gains were seen in the polarized training group. Their time to exhaustion in the incremental run test (or bike test, for nonrunners) increased by a whopping 17.4 percent, compared to 8.8 percent in the high-intensity group, 8 percent in the high-volume group, and 6.2 percent in the threshold group. Maximum speed in the incremental run test (or maximum power in the bike test) increased by 5.1 percent in the polarized group, 4.4 percent in the high-intensity group, and 1.8 percent in the threshold group, and actually decreased by 1.5 percent in the high-volume group. These results are summarized in Table 3.1.

What do the findings of the Salzburg study teach us? Two things: First, they teach us that high-intensity training is essential, but that a little goes a long way. The two groups that completely avoided the high-intensity zone experienced the least improvement. But the group that did the most high-intensity work improved less than the polarized group, which did 2.5 times more training at low intensity than at high intensity.

The other key lesson of this study is that athletes generally get more out of time spent at low intensity than they get out of time spent at moderate intensity. The subjects in the polarized group had the greatest imbalance between low-intensity and moderate-intensity training, and again, they improved the most. This lesson in particular should hit home with recreationally competitive runners, who typically do almost half of their training at moderate intensity.

You may have noticed that the group that came closest to doing 80 percent of its training at low intensity (the high-volume group, at 83 percent) did not improve as much as the polarized group, which did only 68 percent of its training below the ventilatory threshold. Don't get tripped up by this fact. All it really tells us is that doing 80 percent of your running at low intensity won't take you very far if you *never* run at high intensity. Also, it's worth noting that the athletes in the polarized group were supposed to have done about 74 percent of their training at low intensity, not

68 percent, but as in Esteve-Lanao and Seiler's 2013 study, many of the athletes in this group sometimes slipped into the moderate-intensity range when they weren't supposed to. It would be interesting to know if those athletes in the polarized group who spent the most time at low intensity experienced the greatest gains in performance (at least one subject did reach the 80 percent mark), as was the case in Esteve-Lanao and Seiler's 2013 study.

There will be many more studies to come in this fascinating line of research, and they will further clarify our understanding of how to train most effectively for the sport of running. But already we know enough to train more effectively than we ever have before. Today there are still coaches who place a heavy emphasis on high-intensity training. It is now clear that this is a mistake. Other coaches advocate lots of moderate-intensity training, which is how most recreationally competitive runners train anyway. We can now say with certainty that this is a mistake as well. Thanks to the pioneering work of Stephen Seiler, Jonathan Esteve-Lanao, and others, we know the best method is aiming to do 80 percent of our training at low intensity and devoting a fair portion of the remaining 20 percent to high-intensity efforts.

HOW 80/20 RUNNING IMPROVES FITNESS

We have now seen compelling evidence that the 80/20 method of training increases fitness more effectively than other methods do. But how does it actually work? The 80/20 Rule's pioneer, Stephen Seiler, is careful not to claim that this question has yet been fully answered. "While we can say with a high degree of confidence that 80/20 training works," he told me, "we still cannot precisely explain why it works. So this is still an area for research to be done."

Seiler and his colleagues have proposed a few possible explanations for the superiority of 80/20 training that they plan to test in future studies. One possibility is that low-intensity training is more beneficial than it has been given credit for, especially when done in large amounts. Another theory is that runners actually get more benefit from high-intensity training when they do most of their training at low intensity. A third hypothesis is that both moderate- and high-intensity training are too stressful to be done in large amounts.

These explanations are not mutually contradictory, and it may turn out that they are all correct. Indeed, existing evidence strongly indicates that 80/20 training is more effective than other methods for all three reasons.

AEROBIC CAPACITY AND PERFORMANCE

The physiological cornerstone of running performance is aerobic capacity, or the body's ability to extract oxygen from the environment and use it to release energy from muscle fuels. The human aerobic system includes the heart and lungs, the arteries and capillaries that deliver blood to the muscles, the blood itself, and mitochondria, which are little "factories" within muscle cells where oxygen is used to release energy from metabolic fuels. Running induces changes in all of these organs that serve to increase aerobic capacity.

The key requirement for strengthening the aerobic system is stress. Unless you subject your aerobic system to a significantly greater challenge than it faces when you are at rest, it will not adapt. Specifically, you need to elevate your heart rate to at least 60 percent of maximum. So, if your maximum heart rate is 185 beats per minute (BPM), you must run fast enough to get your heart rate up to roughly 111 BPM to boost your aerobic fitness.

While 60 percent of maximum heart rate is the minimum threshold for aerobic benefit, increasing the intensity beyond that threshold brings additional benefits. Research has repeatedly demonstrated that high-intensity exercise strengthens the aerobic system faster than does low-intensity exercise. In one recent study, scientists at McMaster University looked at the effects of exercise intensity on mitochondrial protein synthesis inside muscle cells. These proteins are used to create fresh mitochondria so the muscles can use oxygen more rapidly to fuel their work. The faster these proteins are synthesized, the more densely packed with mitochondria the muscle cells become. The McMaster University researchers discovered that a single high-intensity workout increased mitochondrial protein synthesis significantly more than a low-intensity workout over a period of twenty-four hours.

The same pattern holds when scientists look at other parts of the aerobic system, such as the heart. Research has shown that high-intensity exercise increases the contraction force, or power, of the heart muscle more effectively than does low-intensity exercise.

However, there are some things that low-intensity exercise does better. For example, a number of studies have shown that during prolonged running at low intensity, the muscles release large amounts of a cell signaling compound called interleukin-6 (IL-6), which contributes to fatigue. Well-trained runners produce less IL-6, and this is one reason they are more fatigue resistant. It is believed that exposure to large amounts of IL-6 during running is itself the primary trigger of physiological adaptations that reduce IL-6 release in future workouts and boost endurance. In turn, the primary trigger for IL-6 release is depletion of glycogen fuel in the working muscles. Long, slow runs cause much higher levels of glycogen depletion—and hence also of IL-6 release—than do short, fast runs. A hard run lasting sixteen minutes may increase IL-6 levels twofold. A one-hour run will increase them tenfold, and a full marathon a hundredfold.

So the effects of low-intensity and high-intensity exercise on the aerobic system are somewhat complementary. Maximizing aerobic capacity therefore requires that a runner do some of both. The question, then, is not whether one is "better" than the other and thus ought to be done exclusively. The question, rather, is how high-intensity and low-intensity training should be balanced.

Physiological evidence suggests that the amount of low-intensity training a runner does both *can* and *should* be high. It *can* be high because low-intensity running is not extremely stressful, so a runner really has to go overboard with slow running to reach the point of overtraining. The amount of low-intensity training a runner does also *should* be high because the benefits of low-intensity running continue to accumulate for a long time as the volume of such training increases.

Some runners are skeptical that slow running can possibly continue to be beneficial once they've already gotten in pretty good shape. After all, as I've stated, strengthening the aerobic system requires that some stress be applied to it, and slow running isn't very stressful for experienced runners. But the stressfulness of running is not strictly determined by intensity. Rather, it is determined by the *volume of intensity*. Sure, a thirty-minute run at low intensity applies little stress to a fit individual and thus may provide no benefit in isolation. But a two-hour run at low intensity probably will challenge the aerobic system of any runner, especially if the runner in question ran an hour or so the day before.

Research shows that low-intensity training is truly a gift that keeps on giving. The more slow running you do—up to a point, of course—the more you get in return. Let's return to our example of interleukin-6. As I mentioned above, the farther a person runs, the more fitness-boosting IL-6 his muscles release, while the fitter a person becomes, the less IL-6 the muscles release in a run of any given distance. A beginner may produce enough IL-6 in a slow thirty-minute run to stimulate positive adaptations, whereas an experienced runner may not. To stimulate further adaptations, this second runner will need to run farther, but she need not run faster—in fact, running faster won't help in this instance because, as we saw above, IL-6 release is affected by the duration of running more than the speed. Alternatively, the experienced runner can run slow more often and get the same effect. Runners release more IL-6 when they start out with semi-depleted glycogen stores, and runners who train frequently are often unable to fully replenish these stores between runs.

High-intensity running is different. While a small amount of high-intensity running is more beneficial to the aerobic system than is a small amount of low-intensity running, larger amounts of faster running offer no additional benefit. In fact, large amounts of high-intensity training are so stressful to the body that they suppress the parasympathetic nervous system, resulting in chronic fatigue and loss of performance. So the sum of what we know about the physiological effects of low-intensity and high-intensity exercise tell us that the optimal combination is one that is weighted heavily toward low intensity.

Studies of the actual effects of different combinations of slow and fast running on aerobic capacity (or VO$_2$max) confirm this expectation. One such study was conducted by Veronique Billat in 1999. Her subjects were eight competitive middle-distance runners who ran six times per week. For the first several weeks of the study period, these runners did all of their runs at low intensity. Then they shifted to a schedule of five low-intensity runs and one high-intensity run per week (or a balance of 83 percent low-intensity workouts and 17 percent high-intensity workouts) for a period of four weeks. Finally, the runners transitioned to a schedule of three easy runs and three high-intensity runs per week (or a balance of 50 percent low-intensity workouts and 50 percent high-intensity workouts) for four weeks.

At the end of each phase of the study—the initial 100/0 phase, the subsequent 83/17 phase, and the final 50/50 phase—the runners completed a VO$_2$max test to measure changes in aerobic capacity. The average VO$_2$max at the end of the first phase was 71.2 (which is quite high). Four weeks later—at the end of the 83/17 phase—the group's VO$_2$max had risen to 72.7, an increase of 1.5 percent. Four weeks after that, at the end of the 50/50 phase, the average VO$_2$max was 70.9, a *decrease* of 2.5 percent from the previous level.

In summary, doing three high-intensity workouts per week was not only less beneficial than doing just one—it was worse than doing none at all. Additional data collected by Billat and her colleagues explained why. During the 50/50 phase of the study, the runners exhibited very high levels of norepinephrine, a stress hormone, immediately after hard running. This finding, combined with a second observation of lower heart rates during intense running, indicated that the parasympathetic nervous system of these runners was suppressed. They were overtrained.

Other studies support Billat's finding that the aerobic system is strengthened most effectively by a combination of lots of low-intensity running and a little high-intensity running. In the previous chapter, I discussed the Salzburg study, which compared the effects of four different blends of low-intensity, moderate-intensity, and high-intensity training on performance in an incremental exercise test. We saw that a polarized training program featuring 68 percent low-intensity training produced the best results.

The authors of the study, Thomas Stöggl and Billy Sperlich, also measured the effects of the four training protocols on aerobic capacity. The winner again was the polarized program, which increased VO_2max by a stunning 11.7 percent in nine weeks. The high-intensity program, which featured 43 percent low-intensity training and 57 percent high-intensity training, increased VO_2max by only 4.8 percent.

It bears mentioning that the training plans given to both of these groups were in fact polarized. In other words, both groups were required to avoid the moderate-intensity range. The only difference in their training was the balance of work done at low and high intensities. In relation to the polarized group, therefore, athletes in the high-intensity group were actually *hurt* by doing 57 percent of their training at high intensity versus 24 percent. Beyond that point, each minute they spent at high intensity instead of low intensity worsened their results.

It's also important to recognize that the two groups in the Salzburg study that did the most *moderate-intensity* training—the high-volume group and the threshold group—fared worst of all. Subjects in the threshold group, for example, did 54 percent of their training at moderate intensity, which again is close to what most recreationally competitive runners do, and they experienced a 4.1 percent *decline* in VO_2max. Stephen Seiler sometimes refers to moderate-intensity training as the "black hole" of training intensities because it is almost as stressful as high-intensity training while being far less stimulative of aerobic development. So runners must be at least as wary of sabotaging their training with excessive moderate-intensity running as they are of overcooking themselves with too much speed work.

AEROBIC CAPACITY AND FATIGUE RESISTANCE

A high aerobic capacity is not intrinsically beneficial. No prizes are awarded for VO_2max numbers. The reason runners covet a high aerobic capacity is that it contributes to running performance in a couple of ways. Before we get to that, let me first explain what a higher aerobic capacity will *not* do for you, and that is make you *faster* in any pure sense. In fact, maximizing your aerobic capacity through optimal training will actually make you a *slower* sprinter over short distances.

It is a little-known but well-proven fact that developing the aerobic system reduces top-end speed. Some of the training-induced changes in muscle function that boost performance in, say, a 5K race actually impair performance in something like a 40-yard dash. For example, training to increase aerobic capacity reduces the cross-sectional size of certain muscle fibers. This adaptation leads to economical running over long distances, but it also lessens the maximum power output of the muscles, and as maximum power output goes down, so docs top-end speed.

Exercise scientists sometimes use a vertical jump test to measure the maximum power output of the leg muscles. This test is a good predictor of sprint performance because sprinting is really a form of lateral maximum-power jumping. One study found that vertical jump performance declined by close to 2 percent in college cross-country runners over the course of a season. It is probable that these runners lost an equivalent amount of top-end speed.

What's more, training for increased aerobic capacity also reduces *anaerobic capacity*, or the ability of the muscles to burn fuel quickly without oxygen in support of intense efforts one notch below a full sprint. Exercise scientists typically measure anaerobic capacity with a Wingate test, where subjects are required to pedal as hard as they can for thirty seconds on a stationary bike.

(Power output invariably declines after the first five or ten seconds, which is what distinguishes this test from a test of all-out speed.) The average healthy college student performs better in the Wingate test than does the typical college cross-country runner. And the typical college cross-country runner himself would perform better in a Wingate test after a two-month break from training.

In his famous *Sports Illustrated* article from 1962, Arthur Lydiard argued that distance runners do not need to increase their maximum speed. He was right about that. But it turns out that runners *can't* increase their maximum speed if they train for increased aerobic capacity. Sacrificing VO_2max for raw speed would be a giant mistake for any distance runner, because boosting aerobic capacity through optimal training offers two benefits that matter much more to this type of athlete: 1) it increases the speed that runners can sustain over longer distances; and 2) it increases how far runners can go at submaximal speeds. It is no accident that in the Salzburg study, the training program that induced the largest increase in aerobic capacity (polarized) also yielded the greatest improvements in time to exhaustion and in the highest speed attained in an incremental exercise test.

Aerobic metabolism is more efficient and less fatiguing than other ways the muscles have of powering themselves. The more oxygen your muscles are able to use to fuel your running, therefore, the faster you can run over long distances and the farther you can run at race speeds. Interestingly, increases in aerobic capacity are associated with much larger gains in fatigue resistance (the sustainability of speed) than in speed over distance. I'll show you how with an example.

The average VO_2max of a young adult female is about 38 ml/kg/min. For males, it's about 42 ml/kg/min. According to the exercise physiologist Jack Daniels, a runner with average running economy (a topic I'll address in the next chapter) and a VO_2max of 49 ml/kg/min is likely to be able to run 5K in 20:18, or 6:32 per mile. Now let's suppose that, through smart (80/20) training, this runner eventually increases her VO_2max to 56. According to Daniels, it's likely that this runner will now be able to run 5K in 18:05, or 5:49 per mile. That's an improvement of 10.9 percent in speed over the 5K distance. But this same runner, by lifting her VO_2max from 49 to 56, will now be able to run a marathon in 2:53:20, or 6:36 per mile, which is very close to her original 5K pace. A marathon is 8.5 times longer than a 5K. So the same increase in aerobic capacity that improves "speed over distance" by 10.9 percent elevates the sustainability of speed by *850 percent*.

The giant disparity in the scale of the two main benefits of increased aerobic capacity gives us reason to suspect that improved fatigue resistance in runners is not entirely accounted for by gains in VO_2max. This suspicion is supported by studies in which runners lose fitness instead of getting fitter. For example, in a study conducted by Danish researchers in 1985, well-trained endurance athletes were asked to reduce their training volume from between six and ten hours per week down to just thirty-five minutes per week for four weeks. At the end of that four-week period, their VO_2max was unchanged but their time to exhaustion at 75 percent of VO_2max had dropped by 21 percent. The athletes had lost a ton of fitness, specifically fatigue resistance, but you wouldn't have guessed it from looking at their aerobic capacity.

Gains in aerobic capacity do in fact account for the bulk of the improvement in performance that newer runners experience. It doesn't take long, though, to raise VO_2max as high as it will ever go. Yet runners often continue to lower their race times for many years after their aerobic capacity has plateaued. At the elite level, runners who take up the sport in high school typically attain their lifetime peak VO_2max by their second year of college. Their best race times, however, often don't come until a full decade later.

Consider the example of Paula Radcliffe, one of the greatest female runners of all time. Andrew Jones of Manchester Metropolitan University tracked changes in Radcliffe's physiology and performance from 1991, when Radcliffe was seventeen years old, until 2003, when she was the best female distance runner in the world. Her highest VO_2max was recorded at the very beginning of this period. At that time Radcliffe was running twenty-five to thirty miles per week and her best time for 3000 meters was 9:23. Five years later she was running more than one hundred miles per week and her best 3000-meter time was 8:37, yet her VO_2max was no higher (in fact, it was slightly lower).

What had changed was Radcliffe's ability to sustain the speed she'd always had over longer distances. By 2003, she was running as much as 160 miles per week on an eight-day cycle that included fifteen runs, twelve of which (or 80 percent) were done at low intensity. Her VO_2max was still unchanged, but in that year, she set a still-standing marathon world record of 2:15:25 and ran a half marathon at an average pace of 5:00 per mile, or 2 seconds per mile faster than the pace she had run for 3000 meters (less than two miles) when her VO_2max was at its peak.

While Paula Radcliffe was an exceptional runner in terms of performance, she was not exceptional in terms of how she improved. Runners of all ability levels routinely become more fatigue resistant and thereby lower their race times without increasing their aerobic capacity. Indeed, in the Salzburg study, members of the threshold group increased their time to exhaustion in the incremental exercise test by 8 percent despite the 4.1 percent decline in VO_2max they experienced.

Such research evidence supports real-world evidence from the likes of Paula Radcliffe that the long-term improvements in fatigue resistance runners get from proper training come largely from a source other than increased aerobic capacity. Scientists have recently learned that this other source of fatigue resistance is centered in the brain—and, like aerobic capacity, it is enhanced most effectively by low-intensity, high-volume training. Let's now see how it works.

THE PSYCHOLOGY OF FATIGUE RESISTANCE

From the time it was first identified by Archibald Hill in the 1920s, aerobic capacity was erroneously considered the be-all and end-all of endurance performance. The reason for the mistake had to do with how aerobic capacity was measured. The traditional VO_2max test ties together oxygen consumption and fatigue in an artificial way that gives the appearance that aerobic capacity is the one and only factor limiting endurance performance. Modified versions of the test that do away with this problem reveal that a brain-based tolerance for suffering plays as big a role as aerobic capacity does in relation to fatigue resistance.

The traditional method of measuring a runner's VO_2max is known as a graded exercise test. In this test, the subject runs on a treadmill while breathing into a mask connected to a machine that collects exhaled gases and uses them to calculate oxygen consumption. The speed of the treadmill is increased by a fixed amount every two minutes until the subject quits in exhaustion. Sometimes a subject's oxygen consumption increases in lockstep with his or her running speed right up to the point of quitting. Other times oxygen consumption plateaus a step or two before the runner quits. In either case, the design of the test ensures that the highest recorded rate of oxygen consumption falls close to the point of quitting, making it seem as though nothing else besides the ability to consume more oxygen prevents exhaustion.

The traditional VO_2max test protocol does not resemble how people exercise in the real world. In a race, runners cover a predetermined distance as quickly as possible. This is known as a closed-loop task. By contrast, in a standard VO_2max test, runners choose their own finish line by quitting when they feel they cannot continue any longer. That's an open-loop task.

Exercise scientists overlooked this discrepancy for decades before some of them finally began to wonder what difference a closed-loop VO_2max test might make. In 2010, Lex Mauger and

Nick Sculthorpe at the University of Bedfordshire, England, created one. The Mauger-Sculthorpe test is fixed at ten minutes in length. Those ten minutes are divided into two-minute stages. Whereas in a conventional VO_2max test the treadmill speed is increased by a predetermined amount every two minutes, in the Mauger-Sculthorpe protocol, subjects are instructed to adjust their own speed to attain incrementally increasing ratings of perceived effort. The last two minutes are run at the highest level of effort the subject can tolerate, much like the last two minutes of a race.

Mauger and Sculthorpe got an unexpected result when they compared their test against the traditional VO_2max test. On average, the subjects' VO_2max scores were 8 percent higher in the new, closed-loop test than they were in the standard, open-loop test. Why? The authors speculated that the difference was *motivation.*

Human beings are task-oriented by nature. In the Mauger-Sculthorpe test, subjects know where the end is before they start. They have a specific goal, which motivates them to work harder. In the traditional test, subjects are given only the prospect of ever-increasing misery until they raise a white flag of surrender. That's less motivating.

Runners are generally quite willing to suffer, but they need a reason. In a race or other closed-loop task, they have something to suffer for. In a traditional VO_2max test, they seemingly suffer just to suffer, and it feels unnatural.

If this motivation-based explanation is correct, then performance in a conventional VO_2max test is not limited by physiology, as it was always assumed to be, but rather by psychology. Other evidence suggests that running performance is *always* limited by psychological factors, even in closed-loop tasks such as races. For example, studies have found that when subjects are injected with a drug that makes exercise feel easier, their performance in a race simulation improves. This wouldn't happen unless athletes normally completed races with reserve physical capacity despite feeling as though they've given it their all.

There is an emerging consensus among exercise scientists that runners and other endurance athletes invariably encounter a limit to how much suffering they are willing to tolerate before they encounter any hard physical limit (such as their *true* VO_2max). In the past, scientists believed that exhaustion was strictly caused by physiological factors such as acidosis brought on by insufficient oxygen supply to the muscles. But this idea is contradicted by the fact that runners reach exhaustion at varying levels of muscular acidosis depending on the circumstances. The same is true for muscle glycogen depletion and for every other physical limit believed to cause fatigue. Runners are seldom in precisely the same physiological state at the point of exhaustion in separate tests. The only factor that predicts exhaustion perfectly every time is perceived effort: Athletes always *feel* they cannot continue when they quit, regardless of their physiological status.

This does not mean that tolerance for suffering itself is immovable. As we've already seen in relation to the different VO_2max testing protocols, motivation affects a runner's ability to suffer. Other research has shown that runners perform better in competitive fitness tests than they do in solo fitness tests. When quitting means losing, runners suddenly discover they are able to suffer a little more than they previously felt they could.

Tolerance for suffering is also trainable. Once a runner has discovered that she can suffer more than she thought she could, her perception of effort changes in a lasting way. This was shown in another study involving a closed-loop VO_2max test. Subjects first completed a conventional open-loop test and then, on a separate occasion, they underwent a closed-loop test. On average, their VO_2max scores were 4.4 percent higher in the closed-loop test. Finally, the subjects went back and repeated the conventional VO_2max test. This time they were able to attain the same level of oxygen consumption as in the closed-loop test.

The trainability of suffering tolerance may account for a big chunk of the gains in fatigue resistance and race performance that runners achieve through years of consistent training. Studies suggest this process starts on day one, before a newbie runner has even had a chance to get fitter. For example, in 2013, a team of New Zealand researchers found that children between the ages of nine and eleven years improved their 800-meter run times significantly in their first four attempts at this distance, without doing any training between trials and without adjusting their initial pacing strategy. They improved simply by learning to better interpret their sense of effort and by exploiting what they learned to dig deeper into their physical reserves.

The same process continues well beyond the point where an experienced runner stops getting fitter. In 2007, Ethiopia's Haile Gebrselassie, then thirty-four years old and sixteen years into his career as a professional runner, set a marathon world record of 2:04:26. The first words out of his mouth afterward were "I can run faster." A year later, Gebrselassie returned to the same event, the Berlin Marathon, and ran exactly one second per mile faster. He wasn't fitter than he'd been twelve months before, and he certainly wasn't younger. He just tried harder.

Low-intensity, high-volume training develops the sort of suffering tolerance that enhances fatigue resistance more effectively than does speed-based training. Fast runs may hurt more, but long runs hurt longer. The slow-burn type of suffering that runners experience in longer, less intense workouts is more specific to racing. Speed-based training teaches the mind to expect a quick end to the discomfort of running in a fatigued state. As hard as Emil Zátopek pushed himself in his epic interval workouts, he was never more than 400 meters away from catching a breather. This must have limited him psychologically in races of 5000 and 10,000 meters (indeed, Zátopek had a reputation for erratic pacing, as though he was unable to sustain a consistent level of effort), and it probably held him back even more in the few marathons he ran. In contrast, low-intensity, high-volume training teaches the mind to accept that it might as well make peace with its suffering because it won't end anytime soon.

You might not think that the different relationships to suffering that are taught by mostly-slow training and speed-based training matter much, but there is proof they do. Some of this proof comes from another experiment conducted by Veronique Billat. In this study, a group of distance runners and a group of sprinters were required to complete a run to exhaustion at a high but submaximal intensity, halfway between the lactate threshold and VO_2max (or roughly 10K race pace). This was a type of challenge that would have been quite familiar to the distance runners from training and competition, but not to the sprinters, who would have been accustomed to shorter, faster efforts.

Even though all of the subjects ran at the same relative intensity, the distance runners gave lower ratings of perceived effort throughout the test. They also gave rosier estimates of how long they felt they could continue at various intermediate points of the run. Billat concluded that the distance runners' high-volume, mostly low-intensity style of training had instilled in them a greater tolerance for the type of suffering that is experienced in middle-distance and long-distance races.

It appears, then, that the approach to training that is taken in the 80/20 method does a better job than does speed-based training of equipping runners with the psychological wherewithal to dig deeper into their physical reserves. But it does more than that. Mostly-slow training also does a better job of strengthening the parts of the brain where tolerance for suffering resides.

THE BRAIN AND FATIGUE RESISTANCE

Runners often observe that very long runs and races are more mentally challenging than shorter ones. There's a reason for this. Studies have shown that prolonged exercise at low intensity fatigues the brain to a much greater degree than does high-intensity exercise that doesn't last as long.

In one such study, subjects were required to hold an isometric contraction of the calf muscles as long as possible at three different intensities: 25 percent, 50 percent, and 75 percent of maximum. On average, the subjects were able to sustain the 25 percent contraction ten times longer than the 75 percent contraction. The primary cause of exhaustion at these two intensities was different as well. Scientists are able to assess the contribution of brain fatigue to overall exercise fatigue by measuring the decline in maximum contraction force of the muscles from pre-workout to post-workout. A bigger decline indicates a more tired brain. In this particular study, the maximum voluntary contraction force of the calf muscles declined by 11 percent in the low-intensity trial, whereas it did not decline at all in the high-intensity trial. These results show that the brain was fatigued after the low-intensity test and therefore unable to activate the muscles as forcefully.

We already know that inducing fatigue in the body through exercise triggers adaptations that make the body more resistant to fatigue in the future. Brain fatigue works the same way. Low-intensity runs lasting long enough to tire out the brain strengthen the parts of the brain that aid fatigue resistance. Shorter, faster runs aren't as effective at fatiguing and strengthening these brain areas, which include the insular and temporal lobes, whose job is to perceive the physical elements of emotional states (such as the discomfort of extreme effort), and the anterior cingulate cortex (ACC), whose job is to resolve internal conflicts (such as the conflict between the desire to keep going and the desire to quit when one is running in a fatigued state). The stronger these areas become, the more slowly a runner's sense of effort will increase in races and workouts and the longer he or she will be able to endure the agony of severe fatigue.

It is important to understand that the duration of exercise matters far more than does the intensity of exercise with respect to the goal of enhancing fatigue resistance in the brain. What counts is not how hard the muscles are working but rather how long the brain is required to stay focused on the task at hand. In fact, research has shown that the brain can be fatigued *at rest* in a way that increases fatigue resistance and physical endurance.

In 2012, Samuele Marcora, an exercise scientist at the University of Kent, tested the effects of sedentary brain training on physical endurance. He created a video game that was designed to fatigue and thereby strengthen the anterior cingulate cortex—the part of the brain that helps runners resist the temptation to quit. Marcora then recruited a bunch of nonathletes as subjects and had half of them play the brain-training game regularly for six weeks while the other half watched documentary films instead. Both groups were instructed not to change their exercise habits during the study period. At the start and end of the study, the two groups completed an endurance test consisting of a stationary bike ride to exhaustion. Incredibly, time to exhaustion increased by an average of 20 percent in the brain-trained subjects, compared to no improvement in the other group.

These results demonstrate that brain fitness makes a major contribution to physical endurance that is completely independent of physiology below the neck. You don't even have to exercise to increase brain fitness and fatigue resistance in endurance exercise. All it requires is sustained mental focus on a cognitively demanding task. Of course, building brain fitness through running itself will improve running performance more effectively than building it outside of running. But since the development of brain fitness requires only prolonged task focus and does not require major strain on the body, long runs at low intensity represent the most effective way to boost the brain's capacity to resist fatigue. This helps explain why runners such as Paula Radcliffe improve so much by running a lot, mostly at low intensity, and why no runner improves as much with speed-based training.

Even in combination, however, brain fitness and aerobic capacity do not entirely account for improvements in running performance. As you will soon see, low-intensity, high-volume training also enhances performance in a way that is altogether separate from the two major components of running fitness.

HOW 80/20 RUNNING IMPROVES SKILL

I magine for a moment that some clever chemist has developed a serum with the power to equalize running fitness among all who ingest it. Just swallow two drops and instantly you have exactly the same amount of running fitness as everyone who has done the same. Now, let's say that you and ninety-nine other runners who have sampled the serum compete in a 10K race. What will happen? Will all of you tie for first place? Not a chance. The reason is that fitness is not the only factor that determines running performance. A separate factor is running *skill*.

To be a skillful runner is to have an efficient stride. The standard measure of stride efficiency is running economy, which is roughly equivalent to automobile fuel economy. Whereas fuel economy is represented as the amount of fuel required to travel a given distance, running economy is represented as the amount of oxygen required to sustain a given speed. All runners become more economical through training, which is to say that they exhibit a trend toward requiring less oxygen to sustain the same speeds.

In the preceding chapter, I described how Paula Radcliffe achieved huge improvements in race performance through de facto 80/20 training. I attributed these improvements largely to gains in brain fitness. But improved skill also played a part. Radcliffe submitted to periodic tests of running economy over the course of her career and was observed to become significantly more efficient as time went by.

Whereas fitness has to do with how certain internal organs such as the heart and the brain function, running skill has to do with how the body moves. There is something special about a skilled runner's movements that gives him or her the ability to run at the same pace as a less skillful runner with less effort. Some coaches believe this "something special" is *good form*, or *correct technique*. In all sports, not just running, the term "technique" refers to gross movement patterns, particularly of the limbs, which are describable in terms of angles, frequencies, and so forth. The elements of correct running technique, according to tradition, include a high stride rate, a low stride length (relative to speed), a midfoot or forefoot foot strike, and minimal vertical oscillation (or bouncing). The typical elite runner has most or all of these stride attributes. The average back-of-the-pack runner, on the other hand, has few or none of them.

Technique-focused running coaches try to instill these characteristics in the strides of runners who lack them, assuming that a slow runner who is able to make his or her stride look more like a fast runner's stride *must* get faster as a result. But this assumption turns out to be false. Research has consistently shown that forced alterations to an individual's natural running form almost always worsen performance instead of improving it.

So, if correct technique is not the "something special" about a runner's movements that constitutes the essence of skillful running, then what is? Arthur Lydiard hinted at an alternative in his celebrated 1962 article in *Sports Illustrated*. That article contained exactly one paragraph on the topic of form. In four short sentences, Lydiard said everything he felt a runner needed to know about the matter.

"Forget about form," he wrote. "If a joker throws his arms around, that's fine, so long as he is fit and relaxed. Then he runs smoother and easier, and form takes care of itself. We want the chap who can run for two or three hours and come back looking as fit as he did when he went out."

This was Lydiard's way of saying that there are lots of great runners who lack textbook form. But all great runners exhibit a subtler quality that we might call *relaxed smooth ease.* Unlike correct technique, this other quality actually matters to performance. The more relaxed a runner's stride is, the more resistant that runner is to fatigue. Whereas good running form can be taught (to no avail), relaxed smooth ease is self-taught, or rather self-learned, emerging naturally through the normal fitness-building process. A low-intensity, high-volume (i.e., 80/20) approach to training is not only the most effective way to build running fitness, but is also the best method of developing relaxed smooth ease, which is the true essence of running skill.

These ideas proved to be remarkably prescient. Only since Lydiard's death in 2004 has science defined relaxed smooth ease and shown that simply running more, without trying to imitate some image of perfect running form, is truly the best way to become a more skillful runner. New studies have demonstrated that relaxed smooth ease is the visible manifestation of an acquired "quietness" in parts of the brain that control the body's movements, a sort of neurological efficiency earned through relentless practice that allows the stride to be more adaptive. The ultimate mark of skillful running is the ability to run with *minimal mental effort.* This quiescence of the brain is distinct from the brain-based tolerance for suffering that I described in the last chapter.

To return to our earlier thought experiment, in a 10K race between serum-doped runners of precisely equal fitness, the winner is likely to be the one who has the quietest brain—and this runner is also likely to be the one who does the most slow running.

THE COST OF "CORRECTION"

Historically, formal technique instruction has had a small place in the sport of running. The reason is that most of the top coaches have shared Lydiard's belief that good form is not the true essence of skillful running. But within the past decade or so, a flood of technique-focused coaches has come into the sport. There are many different schools of running technique instruction, but underneath their disparate labels they aren't much different from one another. Whether they call it Chi Running, the POSE method, Evolution Running, Natural Running, or something else, the coaches who teach "correct" form all have pretty much the same thing in mind when they think about proper running technique: a high stride rate, a low stride length, minimal bouncing, and so forth.

It is not at all difficult to teach a high stride rate or any of these other characteristics to a runner who lacks it. The process is not unlike learning dance steps: The instructor demonstrates, the student imitates, the instructor corrects, and—*boom!*—the dance is mastered. So it is reasonable to assume, as technique-focused coaches do, that teaching a runner to consciously imitate the movements of better runners will make him or her faster. But in this case, what makes sense in theory backfires in practice. Research stretching back more than forty years has consistently demonstrated that forced "corrections" to a runner's natural form almost always worsen running economy instead of improving it.

Take stride length, for example. The effects of changes in stride length on running economy have been extensively studied. The most influential study in this line of research was conducted by Peter Cavanagh in 1982. One of the preeminent biomechanists of his generation, Cavanagh recruited ten runners and had them run at stride lengths ranging from 20 percent greater than their natural stride length to 20 percent less without changing their pace. All ten runners consumed the least oxygen—meaning they were most economical—at precisely their natural stride length. In other words, *any* change to their preferred stride length made them less efficient. Cavanagh concluded that runners either naturally adopt the movement patterns that are most efficient for them or they adapt to their chosen movement patterns so that these patterns become maximally efficient over time.

As for bouncing, in a 2012 study a team of Swedish researchers led by Kjartan Halvorsen supplied a group of sixteen male runners with visual and auditory feedback that was intended to reduce the amount of vertical displacement in their stride. It worked. All of the subjects were able to trim some of the "wasteful" excess bouncing from their stride. Unfortunately, it turned out the extra bouncing wasn't wasteful at all. Changing their natural stride in this way made the runners less, not more, efficient.

The same thing happens when scientists meddle with runners' natural foot strike. One study found that experienced runners who were natural forefoot strikers and those who were natural heel strikers had equal running economy, and that neither group became more economical when forced to switch. While a forefoot running style is commonly regarded as superior, the reality is that a heel striking style is more economical for those runners who come to this form naturally and unconsciously.

Defenders of the notion that there is only one correct way to run insist that all runners can become more efficient if their stride is changed to look more like the ideal. They just need time to adjust to such corrections. It isn't realistic, say these coaches, to expect a runner to become more economical the very instant her form is fixed. Given a chance to practice her new and improved technique, however, she will eventually become more efficient. But the evidence does not support this hope. For example, in a 2005 study, researchers at the University of Cape Town switched sixteen experienced triathletes from a heel strike to a forefoot strike and gave them twelve full weeks to practice their new running style under expert supervision. At the end of those twelve weeks, the subjects were still less economical than they had been with their natural foot strike.

SELF-OPTIMIZATION

The fact that any and all changes to a runner's natural stride worsen performance instead of improving it has caused some scientists to speculate that the stride is a self-optimizing system. In chapter 3, we saw that the sport of running itself is a kind of self-optimizing system where training methods evolve over time to produce ever faster runners. Many experts in biomechanics now believe that each runner's stride automatically becomes more efficient over time so that conscious changes in technique are always unnecessary and usually counterproductive.

Support for this belief comes from children. Young children who have just learned how to run are far less efficient than adults are. There are certain metabolic reasons for this disparity, but there are biomechanical reasons too. In particular, young children tend to overstride, taking steps that are longer than their most energy-efficient stride length. As boys and girls get older, however, their stride evolves to become increasingly efficient. This happens regardless of whether a child becomes a jogger or a competitive runner—playground scampering seems to be sufficient—but it happens more quickly in children who do train as runners. Formal technique instruction, though, does not improve running economy in children any more than it does in adults.

Science has shown that in adults, running economy improves drastically within weeks of the commencement of regular training. In 2012, Sharon Dixon of the University of Exeter, England, measured changes in a number of stride features as well as changes in running economy in a group of ten beginner female runners. These women trained for ten weeks without any technique instruction. They just ran. During that period, their running economy improved by 8.4 percent. This improvement was associated with no fewer than seven subtle changes in the women's stride characteristics. For example, peak dorsiflexion of the ankle tended to occur later in the stance phase of the stride after training than it did before. If you're not entirely sure what this means—well, that's kind of the point. Neither did the participants in the study. They were completely unconscious of the adjustment, and in any case, it is not the kind of thing that can be learned by imitation. Such subtle and complexly coordinated efficiency-boosting stride changes must happen on their own if they are to happen at all.

If the running stride does indeed self-optimize for efficiency, it must do so through a specific biological mechanism. One possibility is that the brain somehow monitors the body's rate of oxygen consumption and "captures" movement patterns that minimize oxygen usage. But the latest research suggests that the stride self-optimizes through an entirely different mechanism. A 2012 study found evidence that the brain in fact monitors *muscle activation* and latches onto patterns that yield equal speed with less muscle work—a process that would reduce the oxygen cost of running as a side effect.

This finding lines up with research in other endurance sports, which suggests that it is not oxygen usage but muscle work that the body seeks to minimize in its pursuit of more efficient movement. For example, cyclists naturally adopt a pedaling cadence that does not quite minimize oxygen consumption but does minimize muscle activation. While muscle activation and oxygen consumption are linked, such that they tend to increase and decrease together, they are not identical. Most exercise scientists continue to treat oxygen consumption as the definitive marker of running economy, but if it's true that muscle activation is the true object of the brain's monitoring efforts, then the use of oxygen consumption as a proxy for running skill may be misleading at times.

Whatever the mechanism is by which the running stride evolves toward greater efficiency, it is not open to conscious manipulation. No runner can reduce the number of muscle fibers he or she uses to sustain a given running speed through an act of will. I mean, what would you do if you were running along and a coach shouted out, "Okay, keep going at that pace, but do it by recruiting less total muscle mass"?

If the running stride is truly self-optimizing, though, then why don't all experienced runners look exactly the same when they run? Because no two runners have the same body. Each human body is unique in its structure and neuromuscular wiring. Consequently, while all runners automatically become more economical by reducing muscle activation, all runners do not reduce muscle activation in the same manner. A certain degree of convergence in running form does occur as runners gain experience. For example, as I mentioned above, most runners shorten their stride unconsciously through practice. But even the best runners in the world retain idiosyncrasies that defy the standard image of correct form. Meb Keflezighi, winner of the 2009 New York City Marathon and the 2014 Boston Marathon, is a heel striker. Ryan Hall, American record holder in the half marathon, is bouncy, exhibiting more than twice as much vertical displacement as other elite runners. Mo Farah, winner of five Olympic and world championship gold medals at 5000 and 10,000 meters, takes just 160 steps per minute—far fewer than the 180 that is considered ideal. Technique-focused coaches look at these runners and wrongly think, "Wow! Imagine how much better they would be if they only fixed their form!" Other coaches look at the same runners, as Arthur Lydiard did, and correctly conclude that there must be a difference between "good form" and skillful running.

THE FREEDOM FACTOR

When we characterize an individual runner's stride in terms of qualities such as stride rate, stride length, and vertical displacement, an important feature is overlooked: variability.

No two strides taken by an individual runner are identical. Like a snowflake, each stride is slightly different from any other stride taken by the same runner. If you watch a runner gliding along at a steady pace on a smooth, level surface, it may appear as though every stride is the same, but sensitive instruments such as accelerometers can pick up small variations in movement patterns that the naked eye can't.

Some runners exhibit greater variability in their stride than others do. Generally, experienced runners and fitter runners have the most variable strides, beginners the least. This might seem counterintuitive. You might have supposed that a runner's stride would become *less* variable as he or she became fitter and more experienced, but in fact the opposite happens. This phenomenon is not unique to running. Athletes in all sports become more varied in their movement patterns as they become more skillful.

Variation in the running stride is best thought of as a kind of freedom of movement, or looseness. Could it be that the extra looseness that exists in the strides of fitter and more experienced runners is the very quality that coaches like Arthur Lydiard have perceived as relaxed smooth ease? I believe it is. But where does this freedom come from, and why does it increase automatically with experience and fitness?

The answers to these questions, as I've already hinted, are to be found in the brain. Muscle fibers are activated by the brain. Before the brain activates a collection of muscle fibers to perform a specific motor task, it first creates a mental plan, or blueprint, for the action. Scientists now have the ability to take snapshots of the brain during this planning stage, just before a movement is initiated. What they have found is that the brain never creates the same plan for the same action twice. No matter how basic and familiar the movement is, the brain creates a slightly different plan for it each time the act is performed. This suggests that the brain is simply *unable* to perfectly duplicate any given movement plan. If this is true, it can only be because nature *wants* our movements to be variable. Inconsistency in movements such as running must be somehow beneficial.

The inability of the brain to precisely re-create a plan for a movement such as the running stride explains why no two strides taken by any single runner are ever the same. But it does not explain why some runners exhibit more variability than others do, or why variability tends to increase with experience. The explanation for these patterns has to do with how the brain changes in the process of practicing a motor skill. Brain imaging studies have revealed that several areas of the brain that are highly active during the initial phase of learning a new motor skill—including the cerebellum, premotor cortex, basal ganglia, presupplementary motor area, and supplementary motor area—become less active as skill increases. Other brain regions become more active, but the overall pattern of brain activity over the course of the motor learning process has been characterized as "specific increases with global decreases."

As practice continues, parts of the brain whose job is to represent the particular body parts that are involved in the task actually grow. Additionally, myelin—a sheath of fatty insulating material—forms around the neural connections that are most often used in the task, improving signal transmission. As these structural changes unfold, brain activity during task performance becomes less diffuse and more synchronized, hence more efficient.

Experienced and skilled athletes in all sports exhibit less brain activity, or what I call a quieter brain, than others do when performing sport-specific actions. And, as I mentioned earlier, experienced and skilled athletes in all sports also exhibit more variation in their movements. These two phenomena are linked. Experienced and skilled athletes exhibit more variation in their movements *because* their brain is quieter. The harder the brain is working to control movements, the more constrained those movements become. Better athletes don't have to exert as much mental effort to control their sport-specific movements, so their movements are freer.

Perhaps an analogy will make this idea more understandable.

Think of a novice athlete's brain as being like a supervisor who micromanages his staff. Employees who work under a microman- ager tend to conform to a rigid standard of behavior in response to their boss' constant meddling. Similarly, a novice athlete's movements tend to be rigidly repetitive as a consequence of the brain's intensive efforts to control the body. In contrast, an expe- rienced athlete's brain is like a hands-off supervisor. Employees who work under a laid-back boss tend to bring different styles to the performance of their duties. Analogously, the loose control of the body's movements that is exerted by an experienced ath- lete's brain allows the limbs to move more freely, hence more variably from one repetition to the next. In runners, a quiet brain yields a subtle play in the stride that observers may perceive as a sort of effortlessness.

So we've clarified the relationship between a quiet brain and a more variable stride, or relaxed smooth ease. But one important question remains unanswered: Why are these things good? In other words, precisely how does a runner benefit from having a quieter brain and a looser stride? To answer this question I must enlist the help of robots.

A LESSON FROM ROBOTS

One of the most important insights that scientists have gained con- cerning how humans run (and walk) has come out of efforts to create robots that are able to walk and run like humans. The first two-legged walking machine was created in 1893. This machine was indeed a machine, not a robot, because it was entirely me- chanical and did not contain an internal computer that controlled its movements. It wasn't until 1966 that the first computer-con- trolled two-legged walking robot was built. This invention simu- lated human locomotion better than any mere walking machine because the computer that controlled its movements assumed the role that the human brain executes in walking and running.

Nevertheless, there were important differences between the actions of the first walking robots and real human locomotion. One difference was that robot walking was completely nonadaptive. The first walking robots could do only what they were programmed to do in exactly the way they were programmed to do it. They could not learn to do it better or alter their movements in response to changes in their environment (such as encountering a slope). Also, the movements of the first walking robots just didn't *look* human. They were missing a certain grace and fluidity.

Engineers tried to solve these problems by creating robots with greater and greater computational power. The idea was to preprogram the robots with a rote reaction to every circumstance they could possibly encounter. The best robots of this type were capable of performing thousands of calculations per millisecond in an effort to exert total control over their movements. But it was all for naught. No matter how sophisticated a robot's movement program was, it could never attain true adaptability in this way. And the resources required of the attempt to exert total control were immense. If a living creature had to put so much effort into ambulating, it would never survive in a natural world that rewards efficiency and ruthlessly punishes waste.

Then some engineers had another idea. They went back to a concept first proposed by a Russian neurophysiologist named Nikolai Bernstein in the 1930s. Bernstein believed that most of the work of coordinating the body's movements during locomotion was done not by the brain itself but rather by reflexes located throughout the body. The brain was involved only at an executive level—making decisions about which direction to turn and how fast to go and responding to novel circumstances that the reflexes were not prepared for. Based on this concept, roboticists developed the robot equivalent of a quiet brain, which controlled movements loosely instead of rigidly.

In 2008, the German computational neuroscientist Florentin Wörgötter unveiled RunBot, a walking and running robot whose movements were controlled by a few simple rules that left plenty of room for adjustments based on feedback from sensors positioned at key locations in the robot's body. Unlike its predecessors, RunBot was able to learn on its own how to do things it had not been explicitly programmed to do—such as walk up and down slopes—and its movements were decidedly more graceful. Subsequent designs, including DARPA's Petman, have taken the quiet brain approach further, yielding movements that are increasingly adaptive, efficient, and lifelike.

The lesson that the RunBot breakthrough taught scientists about human locomotion was that loosely controlled movements allow for improvement, whereas rigidly controlled movements do not. A robot that adapts its movement patterns based on feedback about the environment from its body may start off moving less skillfully than a robot that was programmed to exhibit "perfect" form, but in the end, it will be more skillful because it can learn and its rival can't. Likewise, in human runners, a more loosely controlled stride is better able to self-optimize for greater efficiency.

While all beginners tend to be highly conscious of their stride and therefore more rigid in their movements, there is a spectrum. Runners who start off with a little more natural play in the stride become more efficient faster. This pattern holds for all motor tasks, not just running. Yohsuke Miyamoto of Harvard University, himself a former world-class swimmer, has demonstrated that individuals who exhibit greater movement variability when initially performing an unfamiliar hand-eye-coordination task are able to improve faster than those who exhibit less variation.

The adaptability that comes with loosely controlled movements not only facilitates short-term and long-term skill improvement, but it also has an immediate positive effect on efficiency. The overall circumstances in which motor skills such as the running stride are performed are fluid. They are never precisely the same from one moment to the next. Therefore continuous adaptation in movement patterns is required to maintain a high level of efficiency.

Between one run and the next, a runner's body changes in small ways that demand small degrees of adaptation in the stride. In fact, even within a single run, there is a need to adapt. Your body is not the same at the five-mile mark of a moderate-intensity threshold run as it was at the beginning. For this reason, the stride pattern that is most efficient for you when you're fresh is no longer optimal when you're tired. If you have a quiet brain that is receptive to external feedback, you will be better able to adapt your stride to fatigue in order to maintain your stride's efficiency.

This was demonstrated in a 2007 study conducted by Iain Hunter at Brigham Young University. Sixteen experienced runners were asked to run for one hour on treadmills at a challenging pace. Hunter's team measured the stride rates of the runners near the beginning of the run, when they were fresh, and near the end, when they were tired. A runner's stride rate usually decreases as fatigue increases, and that's what happened in this experiment. Exercise scientists have tended to assume that this change is a bad thing—a sign that fatigue is causing a runner's form to deteriorate. Hunter had another suspicion. He hypothesized that the change in stride rate was in fact a spontaneous adaptation to fatigue that served to *preserve* efficiency. Turned out he was right. At both measurement points in the run, Hunter required the subjects to run at each of five different strides rates: their natural stride rate, 4 and 8 percent above their natural stride rate, and 4 and 8 percent below their natural stride rate. He discovered that the runners' natural stride rate was most efficient at both points even though their natural stride rate decreased over the course of the run.

Here is powerful evidence that efficient running is about the brain listening to the body more than it is about the brain telling the body what to do. If the runners in this study had made a conscious effort to maintain their original stride rate throughout the run in spite of mounting fatigue, they would have spoiled their efficiency. Instead they allowed unconscious parts of their brain to adjust the stride in response to fatigue signals from the body and thereby preserved efficiency.

DEVELOPING RELAXED SMOOTH EASE

Becoming a more skillful and efficient runner is more like growing a beard than it is like chopping wood. In other words, you don't make it happen—you allow it to happen. The true essence of skillful running is not correct movements of the limbs but a quiet brain. Therefore the proper goal of all efforts to improve running skill is to reduce brain activity during the act of running. Any measure that helps a runner run more unconsciously is guaranteed to result in better performance. Likewise, any measure that increases brain activation during running will worsen performance.

Consciously altering your natural stride is one such measure. Devoting any more conscious attention to your stride than is strictly necessary is like reverting to an earlier stage in your development as a runner, when the stride action was less familiar and intense self-consciousness was unavoidable.

Numerous studies have shown that people move less skillfully and learn motor tasks more slowly when they are required to focus their attention on their body. A few of these experiments have involved running. A 2009 study by German researchers, for example, found that runners were less economical when thinking about the movements of their body as they ran than they were when focusing on their breathing, and were less economical when focused on their breathing than they were when they paid attention to the environment around them. What's most interesting about these findings is that the runners' biomechanics did not change across the three conditions; only their brain activity changed. So it appears that forced "corrections" to the stride reduce efficiency not only by dislodging runners from the natural movement patterns they have developed through experience but also by forcing runners to think harder about what they're doing.

If consciously changing your natural stride is not the best way to enhance your running skill, then what is? As we saw at the beginning of the chapter, Arthur Lydiard believed that high-volume training was the secret to developing relaxed smooth ease, which he correctly identified as the visible mark of skillful running. Given what we now know about the self-optimizing nature of the stride, we should indeed expect that simply running more would be the surest way to accelerate the acquisition of relaxed smooth ease.

The three key characteristics of a self-optimizing system are variation, selection, and repetition. Variation is built into the neuromuscular system. Because no two strides that you take are exactly the same, each stride constitutes a small experiment. Your next stride may be slightly more efficient than the one before (requiring less muscle activation to sustain the same pace) or slightly less efficient. If it's more efficient, your brain is likely to "select" it, remembering key details of the activation pattern that produced it and incorporating them into the blueprint for your stride, thus making it more efficient generally. Obviously, you can't make much progress toward optimization with a single stride. It takes many thousands of strides to make measurable gains. That's where repetition comes in. High-volume training packs more strides into less time, resulting in faster progress. And keeping the intensity low most of the time—in other words, following the 80/20 Rule—allows you to run more without burning out.

So the best way to become a more skillful runner is identical to the best way to maximize your running fitness. But although relaxed smooth ease comes from the same source that running fitness comes from, it is an entirely separate thing. This was demonstrated in a clever study done by my friend Stephen McGregor, an exercise scientist at Eastern Michigan University. The purpose of this study was to distinguish the effects of high-volume running on fitness from its effects on running skill. To do this, McGregor recruited two groups of subjects: college runners and competitive triathletes. Both groups underwent two kinds of testing. A standard VO_2max test was used to measure the aerobic fitness of the runners and the triathletes. In addition, accelerometers were used to measure the amount of variability, or relaxed smooth ease, in the strides of the two groups.

McGregor found that VO_2max, or fitness, was about the same in the two groups. But the runners exhibited more variability in their stride, indicating that they were more skillful. McGregor attributed these findings to differences in training. The total training loads of the two groups of athletes were comparable, and that's why their fitness scores were roughly the same. But whereas the triathletes divided their training time among three disciplines—swimming, cycling, and running—the runners did nothing but run, and that's why their strides exhibited more relaxed smooth ease. McGregor had proved that the more running a person does, the freer and more efficient his or her stride becomes, independent of changes in fitness. Simply repeating the stride action, over and over, as much as possible, without interference, is the secret to becoming a more skillful runner.

Arthur Lydiard had it right in 1962. If you want a better stride, all you have to do is run enough so that eventually you can run for two or three hours without looking any less fresh at the end than you did at the beginning and your form will "take care of itself." Running at low intensity most of the time (specifically, 80 percent of the time) will enable you to run more so you can take fuller advantage of this natural process.

6.

MONITORING AND CONTROLLING INTENSITY

The 80/20 Rule governs running intensity, which we can define simply as how hard the body is working during a run relative to how hard it is capable of working. To practice 80/20 running effectively, you need to actively monitor and control your intensity throughout every run. Trying to maintain the right balance of training intensities without paying attention to how hard you're working during your runs would be like trying to balance a houschold budget without paying attention to income or expenditures.

There are lots of ways to measure intensity, none of them perfect. For example, exercise scientists commonly use oxygen consumption as an indicator of exercise intensity, but oxygen consumption peaks at running speeds that are well below maximal, so it can't be used to quantify intensity at very high speeds. Beyond that, it's impractical. The required equipment costs a fortune and weighs a ton. Other measures of exercise intensity, including blood lactate concentration, have different kinds of limitations that confine their use to the laboratory.

The three most practical measures of running intensity are perceived effort, heart rate, and pace. Each has its own set of advantages and weaknesses. You will get the best possible results from your 80/20 training if you use all three of them complementarily. In this chapter, I will give you concrete guidelines for monitoring and controlling your running intensity by perceived effort, heart rate, and pace, both individually and in combination.

PERCEIVED EFFORT

Perceived effort is nothing more than how hard you *feel* you're working during a run. This feeling is distinct from other perceptions you experience when running, such as a burning sensation in your windpipe or soreness in your calf muscles. When you're working very hard in the middle of a run, you can sense it even if your windpipe is not burning and there is no pain in your calf muscles. In fact, numbing the legs with anesthesia has no effect on perceived effort. The reason is that perceived effort is literally "all in your head." Studies have demonstrated that effort perception is mainly a function of how hard the brain is working to drive the muscles. In other words, it is the brain's perception of its own effort, not the body's. The harder the brain is driving the muscles, the more intense the effort feels.

Scientists use a measurement called *movement related cortical potential* (MRCP) to quantify how hard the brain is driving the muscles during exercise. A study led by Samuele Marcora at the University of Kent found that both MRCP and subjective ratings of effort were proportionally greater in subjects when they lifted a heavy weight than when they lifted a light weight. This is exactly what we would expect to see if brain activity determined perception of effort.

The same study also found that MRCP and perceived effort were just as high when subjects lifted a light weight with a tired arm as when they lifted a heavy weight with an arm that wasn't tired. Runners can certainly relate to this second finding. If you start running at a full sprint, you will experience a high level of effort immediately, before you get tired. That's because your brain has to drive your muscles very hard when you run fast. On the other hand, when you run slowly, your sense of effort is low initially, but then it increases gradually as you keep going. That's because your brain has to work harder and harder to drive the muscles as they become fatigued. What's more, as we saw in the preceding chapter, the brain itself becomes fatigued during pro- longed low-intensity exercise so that actual stimulation of the muscles by the brain decreases even though the brain is trying harder to keep the body moving.

What all of this means to you is that the relationship between perceived effort and intensity is not a pure one, but is corrupted by fatigue. The effect of fatigue on perceived effort has impor- tant practical implications for the use of this metric to monitor and control running intensity. If you do a long run at a steady pace, your intensity, by definition, will also remain steady, but your perceived effort will increase as fatigue sets in. To keep your effort steady, you will have to slow down somewhat toward the end of the run. This is not the most sensible way to use perceived effort to control running intensity, however. Instead, I suggest you use perceived effort to establish the appropriate intensity at the start of a workout or workout segment. Then rely on pace or heart rate to maintain that intensity while allowing your per- ceived effort to gradually increase as fatigue sets in.

This is not to say that you should ever completely ignore per- ceived effort when running. On the contrary, you must always allow perceived effort to have the final say in controlling the in- tensity of workouts. Even though perceived effort is "all in your head," it tells you how your body is doing in a holistic way that pace and heart rate do not. Any factor that affects your body's capacity in a given moment will alter the relationship between mental effort and physical output in a way that you can perceive. For example, if the quality of your last night's sleep was poor, this might affect your body's capacity in today's run. It will take a greater-than-normal mental effort to produce a normal level of performance, and you'll feel it. Even if you aren't aware that you slept poorly, you'll just feel a little "flat" as you run.

Every runner has occasional flat days in training. Often these days come when you least expect them and have no apparent cause. But there's always a cause, whether it's identifiable or not, and this feeling of flatness is your brain's way of telling you that it has detected something amiss internally and you shouldn't push yourself. On these days, you will experience unusually high effort at any given pace or heart rate. If you force yourself to stick to a preselected pace or heart rate target, you will probably end up feeling even worse the next day. In such circumstances, it's best to trust your brain more than you trust your GPS watch or your heart rate monitor and slow down as much as necessary to keep your perceived effort where it should be.

To get the most benefit from training by perceived effort, you need to quantify it. In chapter 1, I mentioned that scientists use a tool called the Borg Scale of Perceived Exertion to gather ratings of perceived effort from participants in exercise studies. This fifteen-point scale is presented in Figure 6.1. I prefer to use a modified ten-point scale of perceived effort that is easier to use in combination with heart rate and pace monitoring. This scale is presented in Figure 6.2.

The whole point of monitoring intensity in an 80/20 running program, remember, is to ensure that the program properly balances efforts at low, moderate, and high intensity. So the first thing we need to do with these scales of perceived effort is divide them into low-, moderate-, and high-intensity ranges.

There are actually multiple scientific definitions of these three ranges of intensity, but the differences among the competing definitions are small and of no practical consequence. Also in chapter 1, I described a study done by Arizona State University researchers who defined moderate exercise as the range of intensities that fall between the ventilatory threshold, where the breathing rate abruptly increases, and the lactate threshold, where talking becomes uncomfortable. This is the definition of moderate intensity that I have used to formulate guidelines for monitoring and controlling the intensity of workouts in the 80/20 running system, not only by perceived effort but by heart rate and pace as well.

FIGURE 6.1 **THE BORG SCALE OF PERCEIVED EXERTION**

RATING	DESCRIPTION
6	
7	Very, very light
8	
9	Very light
10	
11	Fairly light
12	
13	Somewhat hard
14	
15	Hard
16	
17	Very hard
18	
19	Very, very hard
20	

Clinical testing has shown that runners of all levels consistently rate their effort at or near 12 on Borg's 6 to 20 scale when they are working at the ventilatory threshold. This rating corresponds to a rating of 5 on the 1 to 10 scale that I prefer. At the slightly higher lactate threshold, runners consistently rate their effort between 13 and 14 on Borg's scale, which equates to a rating of just under 6 on the 1 to 10 scale. On this same scale, then, moderate intensity is represented by perceived effort ratings of 5 to 6, low intensity by ratings of 1 to 4, and high intensity by ratings of 7 to 10. Obeying the 80/20 Rule therefore is a simple matter of keeping your perceived effort rating below 5 roughly 80 percent of the time.

Getting the very most out of 80/20 running is a little more complicated, however. While a three-zone system of classifying exercise intensities is adequate for scientific purposes, it is not quite adequate for practical use in training. The reason is that the low- and high-intensity ranges are rather broad. These broad ranges allow too much leeway to run either faster or slower than one should in certain types of workouts that demand fairly precise regulation of intensity.

FIGURE 6.2 TEN-POINT SCALE OF PERCEIVED EFFORT

RATING	DESCRIPTION	INTERNAL CUES	
1	Extremely Easy	"I feel like I could run forever at this pace."	
2	Very Easy	"I feel like I'm really holding myself back."	
3	Easy	"I feel like I'm holding myself back just a little."	
4	Comfortable	"This pace feels natural, like I'm neither holding back nor pushing."	
5	Fairly Comfortable	"I feel like I'm pushing myself ever so slightly."	
6	Slightly Hard	Less fit runners: "I feel like I can keep up this pace for 20 to 30 minutes."	Fitter runners: "I feel like I can keep up this pace for 50 to 60 minutes."
7	Somewhat Hard	Less fit runners: "I feel like I'm going to blow up in 10 to 15 minutes."	Fitter runners: "I feel like I'm going to blow up in 15 to 20 minutes."
8	Hard	"I feel like I can keep this pace up for a mile or so, no more."	
9	Very Hard	"I feel like I can sustain this pace for a couple of minutes, *maybe* three."	
10	Extremely Hard	"I feel like I can only hold this pace for 1 minute, tops."	

In the next section, I will describe a five-zone system of measuring intensity by heart rate. Each of the five zones in this system corresponds to a two-point range of perceived effort, so the two scales fit together nicely. In addition to allowing for more precise control of intensity during workouts, the five-zone system offers a way of enhancing the reliability of perceived effort ratings. Runners who lack experience in rating their perceived effort tend to exhibit an initial tendency to underestimate their true intensity. Monitoring your heart rate with my five-zone system will help you properly calibrate your effort ratings.

For example, Zone 4 corresponds to perceived effort ratings of 7 and 8. During workouts that call for efforts in Zone 4, you can pay attention to how you feel while running within your Zone 4 heart rate range to get a better sense of what perceived effort ratings of 7 and 8 really feel like. In the closing section of this chapter, I will present a table that shows the correspondence between perceived effort, heart rate, and also pace in each of the five intensity zones.

There is some interesting research indicating that estimated time to exhaustion is also a very good subjective indicator of objective running intensity. The idea is simple: You ask yourself, "How long can I keep this up?" and your answer tells you how hard you're working. The "Internal Cues" column of table 6.1 provides information based on this concept that you may find helpful in the process of mastering my 1 to 10 scale of perceived effort.

HEART RATE

Every runner knows from experience that heart rate is a good indicator of exercise intensity. Even if you've never monitored your heart rate during a run, you know that your heart beats harder and faster as your speed increases because you can feel it. This link between the activity of the heart muscle and the activity of the skeletal muscles exists because the harder your skeletal muscles are working, the more oxygen they need, and the faster your heart is beating, the more oxygen-rich blood is circulated through the body.

Like every other aspect of the act of running, the heart rate response to running intensity is controlled by the brain. One part of the brain that is involved in such control is the insular cortex, whose role in fatigue awareness I mentioned in chapter 4. The insular cortex monitors muscle activity and adjusts both the force and the rate of heart muscle contractions to meet the muscles' oxygen needs.

Heart rate is only one among many physiological functions that vary in predictable ways alongside changes in exercise intensity, and it is no more definitive as a marker of intensity than is any other function—it's just easier to measure. Yet heart rate is connected to other physiological processes in ways that make it a particularly useful marker for overall exercise intensity. For example, research has shown that in fit runners, the muscles oxidize fat most rapidly at the heart rate that corresponds to the ventilatory threshold. You can't monitor fat burning in real time on your own when you run, but you can easily monitor your heart rate. So if you want to increase your muscles' ability to burn fat, all you have to do is strap on a heart rate monitor and run at your ventilatory threshold heart rate.

The only catch is that each runner has a different ventilatory threshold heart rate—and a different resting heart rate, maximum heart rate, lactate-threshold heart rate, and so on. There are several factors that shape each runner's personal "heart rate profile." The most important factors are body size (larger individuals typically have lower resting heart rates), age (maximum heart rate tends to decline with age), aerobic fitness (fitter individuals are able to sustain higher heart rates for longer periods of time), and heredity (a number of genes influence resting heart rate, maximum heart rate, and innate aerobic fitness).

Because each runner has a unique heart rate profile, effective heart rate–based training requires that target heart rate zones be individually customized. The lodestar for establishing custom heart rate training zones is the lactate threshold heart rate. In much the same way that identifying magnetic North allows a sailor to "box the compass," identifying the lactate threshold heart rate enables a runner to define a complete set of custom heart rate training zones. In my five-zone scheme, the lactate threshold heart rate marks the upper limit of the moderate intensity range. Heart rates above this number represent high intensity. Heart rates below the ventilatory threshold (which, again, is just a step below the lactate threshold) represent low intensity.

Exercise scientists determine the lactate threshold heart rate of individual runners by having them run at incrementally increasing speeds on a treadmill until the blood lactate concentration is 4 mmol/L. The heart rate at this point is by definition the runner's current lactate threshold heart rate. It's not quite as precise as it sounds, though. A runner who goes through this test five days in a row might get a slightly different result each time, because the body's physiological state changes from day to day.

What's more, the 4 mmol/L standard itself is somewhat arbitrary. It is supposed to mark the exercise intensity at which the blood lactate concentration suddenly spikes, but for many runners, this magic number falls somewhat off the mark. Fortunately, it doesn't matter. Science has shown that runners get equally fit whether they exercise slightly above, precisely at, or slightly below the heart rate that is associated with a blood lactate concentration of 4 mmol/L in their designated moderate-intensity workouts. In other words, close is good enough when it comes to determining the lactate threshold heart rate, and it so happens that it's possible to get close to the scientific standard for identifying the lactate threshold with do-it-yourself alternatives to lab-based testing.

One alternative is a thirty-minute time trial. Here's how it works: Warm up with several minutes of easy jogging and then run as far as you can in thirty minutes while wearing your heart rate monitor. Your average heart rate during the last ten minutes of this effort is your lactate threshold heart rate. The downside of this test is that it's rather painful.

A less taxing option is to determine your lactate threshold heart rate by perceived effort. As I mentioned in the previous section, the lactate threshold heart rate corresponds to a rating of 6 on a 1 to 10 scale of perceived effort. So you can estimate your lactate threshold heart rate by starting a run at a perceived effort of 1 and then increasing your effort point by point until you give it a rating of 6. Your heart rate at this point is your lactate threshold heart rate. The downside of this test is that a little practice is needed to master the art of quantifying subjective effort.

|||||||||||||||||||||||||||||||||||||||||||||||||||||||||||||||||||||||||||||||||||||||||||||||||||||||||||||||

THERE'S AN APP FOR THAT

The perceived effort–based method of determining lactate threshold heart rate is built into an 80/20 Running smartphone app that I developed with PEAR Sports. When you use it, you will be guided through the test with audio cues (you'll actually hear my voice). The app also captures the lactate threshold automatically and uses it to calculate your five personal heart rate training zones. The workout itself is easy enough that you can repeat it the next day if you don't trust your initial result. All of these features make the app-based version of the perceived effort method more reliable than the low-tech version.

|||||||||||||||||||||||||||||||||||||||||||||||||||||||||||||||||||||||||||||||||||||||||||||||||||||||||||||||

Another simple do-it-yourself method of determining the lactate threshold heart rate is the talk test. The lactate threshold heart rate is associated with the fastest running pace at which a runner is able to talk comfortably. While wearing a heart rate monitor, start jogging at a slow, steady pace. After one minute, recite the Pledge of Allegiance (see Figure 6.3) and note your heart rate. Alternatively, count upward from 120 to 125. Now increase your speed slightly, wait a minute, recite the Pledge (or count) again, and again note your heart rate.

Continue in this fashion until talking is slightly uncomfortable. Note your pace at the *previous* speed when speaking was comfortable or sort of comfortable. Your heart rate at that pace is your current lactate threshold heart rate. *Comfortable* in this context does not mean that you are able to talk without feeling any sense of dyspnea, or oxygen deficit, but the feeling should be quite mild. Here's a good rule of thumb: If your breathing returns to its pretalking rhythm by the third breath after you finish speaking, then you were able to talk comfortably. Note that the smaller your speed increases are when you perform this test, the more precise the result will be.

FIGURE 6.3   TALK TESTS

FIGURE 6.3   TALK TESTS

Use either of these talk tests to find the highest running intensity at which you are able to talk comfortably, which marks your lactate threshold.

THE PLEDGE OF ALLEGIANCE	COUNTING
I pledge allegiance to the flag of the United States of America and to the republic for which it stands, one nation under God, indivisible, with liberty and justice for all.	One hundred twenty. One hundred twenty-one. One hundred twenty-two. One hundred twenty-three. One hundred twenty-four. One hundred twenty-five.

Once you've determined your lactate threshold heart rate, you can use it to calculate a full set of target heart rate training zones. Numerous heart rate training formulas exist, most of which are fairly similar to one another. As I mentioned in the previous section, the three-zone systems that scientists use are not adequately partitioned to meet the needs of runners training in the real world. So instead I use a five-zone system that I developed for PEAR Sports. Table 6.1 presents this system along with a specific example of target zones for a runner whose current lactate threshold heart rate falls at 160 beats per minute.

It's easy to line up my five-zone heart rate system and the scientists' three-level hierarchy, as we've done already with respect to perceived effort ratings. Remember that I've chosen to define

TABLE 6.1   5-ZONE HEART RATE TRAINING SYSTEM

ZONE	ZONE NAME	PERCENT OF LACTATE THRESHOLD HEART RATE	TARGET ZONES FOR RUNNER WITH LACTATE THRESHOLD HEART RATE OF 160 BPM
1	Low Aerobic	75–80	120–128
2	Moderate Aerobic	81–89	129–142
3	Threshold	96–100	153–160
4	VO$_2$max	102–105	163–168
5	Speed	106+	169+

low intensity as the range of intensities that fall below the ventilatory threshold, moderate intensity as the range of intensities between the ventilatory threshold and the lactate threshold, and high intensity as anything above the lactate threshold. The ventilatory threshold falls at the bottom end of Zone 3 (or 96 percent of lactate threshold heart rate). The lactate threshold is aligned with the top end of Zone 3 (or 100 percent of lactate threshold heart rate). That's your moderate intensity range. Zones 1 and 2, then, represent low intensity and zones 4 and 5 are high intensity.

By the way, the bottom end of Zone 4—102 percent of lactate threshold heart rate—aligns closely with the respiratory compensation point, which is where 80/20 advocates Stephen Seiler and Jonathan Esteve-Lanao position the dividing line between moderate and high intensity. So the high-intensity range in my system matches theirs.

You've probably already observed that the five zones are not perfectly contiguous. The top end of Zone 2 is 89 percent of lactate threshold heart rate and the bottom end of Zone 3 is 96 percent of lactate threshold heart rate. This buffer exists to ensure that your low-intensity efforts don't ride the fence between low and moderate intensity. On the other side, there is a small gap between the top end of Zone 3 and the low end of Zone 4. This gap exists because 101 percent of lactate threshold heart rate is just a bit too slow for the types of runs that are normally used to target Zone 4.

Each zone has its proper place in a runner's training. Zone 1 is appropriate for warm-ups, cool-downs, recovery periods between high-intensity intervals, and recovery runs. Zone 2 is targeted in what I call foundation runs (which most other coaches call easy runs) and long runs. Zone 3 is targeted in tempo runs, cruise intervals, and fast finish runs. A typical threshold run comprises a steady effort of fifteen to forty minutes in Zone 3 sandwiched between a warm-up and a cool-down. Cruise intervals are like tempo runs except the middle of the sandwich is separated into multiple shorter Zone 3 efforts. A fast finish run is a foundation run with a short (five to fifteen minutes) effort in Zone 3 tacked onto the end. Zone 4 is typically targeted in high-intensity interval workouts featuring longer intervals (two to eight minutes) and in fartlek (or what I call "speed-play") runs, which are simply interval workouts with a less formal structure that are done on roads or trails instead of at the track. Zone 5 is appropriate for high-intensity runs featuring shorter intervals (thirty to ninety seconds), hill repetition runs, and more intense speed-play runs. I will present detailed guidelines for performing all of these workout types in the next chapter.

Note that your lactate threshold heart rate will change somewhat as your fitness level changes, rising slightly as you get fitter and dropping a bit if you should ever lose fitness. Therefore it is necessary to repeat whichever test you use to determine your lactate threshold heart rate and recalculate your heart rate zones periodically to keep them current. You need not do this on any particular schedule, but only as often as you experience a noticeable change in your level of fitness.

Heart rate monitoring is especially useful in low-intensity runs. The reason is that, unlike pace, heart rate is not a performance metric. Runners don't instinctively push to achieve higher heart rates that they can boast about the way they often push to achieve faster split times. When runners are given a heart rate "ceiling" to stay below, they usually have no trouble respecting it. But when they are given a pace target, they often try to beat it.

Many noteworthy runners have used a heart rate monitor primarily to hold themselves back. For example, Paula Radcliffe trained by heart rate in easy runs to keep herself from pushing too hard but trained by pace and time on the track. Ryan Hall began to wear a heart rate monitor in 2013, the year after an ill-advised experiment with frequent high-intensity running resulted in a series of injuries.

Heart rate monitoring is less useful in high-intensity runs. The reason has to do with a phenomenon called cardiac lag. When you speed up during a run, your heart will respond by increasing its contraction rate until it is sufficient to supply your muscles with the extra oxygen they're now asking for. This process is not instantaneous. Depending on how much your pace increases, it may take your heart thirty seconds or more to settle into a new rhythm.

Cardiac lag has important implications for heart rate monitoring during workouts that include changes in pace. For example, suppose you are doing a run that features six intervals of thirty seconds in Zone 5 with two-minute recoveries in Zone 1 between intervals. When you start the first interval, you will accelerate abruptly, and your heart rate will begin to climb. But chances are your heart rate will not actually reach Zone 5 until the very end of the thirty-second interval, if even then. That doesn't mean you failed to do the interval at the right intensity. As long as you were running fast enough that your heart rate would have reached Zone 5 if you had continued at that pace, then you did it correctly.

Likewise, when you slow down for recovery at the end of your first thirty-second Zone 5 interval, your heart rate will begin to decrease. But because of cardiac lag, no matter how much you slow down, your heart rate might not get all the way back down to Zone 1 before your two-minute recovery ends and it's time to start the next interval. Again, this doesn't mean you screwed up. As long as you jogged slowly enough that your heart rate would have dropped down to Zone 1 eventually, you did it correctly.

To avoid getting tripped up by cardiac lag in workouts involving short efforts at high intensity, use perceived effort and pace as your primary intensity metrics in such workouts. Changes in perceived effort are instantaneous, and most running devices with GPS or accelerometer technology register changes in pace within a few seconds. When a given workout calls for a change from high intensity (Zone 4 or 5) to low intensity (Zone 1 or 2) or vice versa, target the appropriate perceived effort or pace as defined by Table 6.2. If the segment lasts long enough for your heart rate to eventually stabilize, you can then use heart rate to confirm that you're in the right zone.

PACE

Pace, which is calculated as time over distance, represents intensity in a way different from perceived effort and heart rate. Exercise intensity is essentially an *input*: It is how much physiological effort the body is putting into running. Perceived effort and heart rate are direct indicators of physiological effort. Pace, on the other hand, measures the performance *output* of that input. This makes pace a reliable indicator of intensity, because there is a direct relationship between how much the body puts into running and the resulting performance output. If you're running faster, it can only be because your body is working harder.

As a performance metric, pace *matters* more than do other indicators of intensity in a crucial sense. When you compete, your pace determines your finish time, and your finish time is the basis for assessing your performance. Heart rates are not included in official race results. No awards are given for the greatest perceived effort.

The basic relevance of pace to performance makes it a great way to measure progress in training. If your average pace or your split times in particular types of workouts improve as the weeks go by, you know your training is going well. If these numbers don't improve, you know something is wrong.

The fact that runners care about pace more than they do about perceived effort ratings and heart rates imbues it with the power to motivate in a way that other intensity metrics do not. When runners are on the clock, they try harder. While it's possible in principle to try hard without wearing a watch, research shows that runners seldom try as hard when running entirely by feel. For example, a 2010 study conducted by researchers at New Zealand's Massey University found that runners completed a 6K time trial 6 percent faster with performance feedback than they did without it.

Seldom, if ever, should you try as hard in workouts as you do in races. Treating workouts like races is a recipe for burnout. But in periods of race-focused training, you should engage in challenging workouts targeting Zones 4 and 5 (high intensity) once or twice per week. If you monitor your pace in these workouts, you will tend to put a little more effort into them and consequently get a little more benefit out of them.

The trick is to push yourself without pushing too hard in these faster runs. The best way to strike this balance is to aim to slightly improve your performance in benchmark workouts as the training process unfolds, instead of aiming to achieve your best possible performance in each of them as you would do in a race. Suppose, for example, that your training plan for an upcoming 10K race includes three workouts featuring three-minute intervals in Zone 4. The first time you do this workout, forget about performance and use perceived effort to monitor and control your intensity, aiming for a rating of 7 to 8 on my ten-point scale. But even though you are not thinking in terms of performance, go ahead and wear a speed-and-distance device during the workout and record your average pace for the intervals.

When you repeat the workout, use pace as your *primary* intensity metric, aiming to run each three-minute interval a second or two per mile faster than you did in the previous workout. (Even though you will run less than a mile in each interval, your pace will still be measured in minutes and seconds per mile.) Since your fitness is improving, your perceived effort should be about the same as it was in the previous session despite the fact that you're running a little faster. When you do the workout a third time, again aim to improve your times, but only very slightly so that the session doesn't take more out of you than it should.

It's important that you complete even your toughest workouts feeling as if you could have run a bit faster or gone a tad farther. When one of your "flat" days happens to coincide with a high-intensity workout, allow perceived effort to have the final say and give up your aim of improving your performance for the sake of completing the workout feeling you could have done more.

In addition to being more performance-relevant than heart rate, pace is free of the lag phenomenon that limits the usefulness of heart rate monitoring in high-intensity workouts featuring short intervals in Zone 4 or 5. So there are really two reasons why pace is the best choice for use as the primary gauge of intensity in high-intensity workouts.

In low-intensity workouts (Zones 1 and 2), pace should *not* be your primary intensity metric. Runners more often derail their progress by consistently running too fast in low-intensity workouts than they do by occasionally running too fast in moderate- and high-intensity workouts. It is natural for runners to want their pace to compare favorably against their normal pace in all kinds of workouts, even easy runs. This disposition seduces runners into pushing a little harder in runs where they should not push themselves than they would if they were not paying attention to the clock. A single lapse of this type does little harm, but a consistent habit of pressing the pace in designated low-intensity runs hampers progress by creating a burden of fatigue that is carried throughout the training process and lowers performance in the workouts that are intended to be more challenging. Establishing individualized target pace zones for different types of workouts, including easy runs, offers a way of avoiding this problem, but it only works if those zones are respected. As I stated earlier, it's been my observation that runners have a harder time obeying "speed limits" in low-intensity runs than they do heart rate limits.

What about moderate-intensity (Zone 3) runs? In the various types of workouts in which moderate intensity is targeted, the Zone 3 efforts last long enough that cardiac lag is not an issue. Monitoring your heart rate during moderate-intensity runs will help you avoid pushing too hard, as it does in low-intensity runs. But moderate-intensity runs often are meant to be challenging, and monitoring your pace in them will motivate you to meet that challenge, as it does in high-intensity runs. So I suggest you use both heart rate and pace to regulate intensity in moderate-intensity runs, while using perceived effort to find the right intensity at the start of each Zone 3 effort (aiming for a rating of 5 to 6) and to make any necessary adjustments as you go, like slowing you down if you're having a flat day.

In order to use heart rate monitoring and pace monitoring interchangeably in moderate-intensity runs, you will need to have a set of five custom pace zones that line up with your five target heart rate zones. You can easily define these pace zones by essentially backing into them through your heart rate zones. Here's how: Once you've established your heart rate zones, complete another test workout to establish matching pace zones. To do this test you will need a device such as the Polar RS300X that is capable of measuring both heart rate and pace.

Be sure to conduct this workout on flat terrain. Begin by jogging very slowly for five minutes. Next, adjust your effort until your heart rate settles into a steady rhythm at the top of your Zone 1 heart rate range. Note your pace. Now increase your effort very slightly until your heart rate is at the bottom of your Zone 2 range. (This will be no more than two BPM higher.) Again, note your pace. Continue in this fashion until your heart rate reaches the bottom end of your Zone 5 range and note the corresponding pace one last time. You now have a full set of pace zones to complement your heart rate zones.

I recognize that many runners are resistant to wearing a heart rate monitor while running and much prefer to train entirely by pace. Either they find the chest strap that most heart rate monitors come with uncomfortable or they have some other objection. While I've made it clear that I believe heart rate monitoring is a better way of regulating intensity in low-intensity runs, I concede that a runner can practice 80/20 running correctly without heart rate monitoring if she respects her Zone 1 and Zone 2 pace ranges. But runners who choose to eschew heart rate monitoring must come up with their five custom pace zones through a different method than the one I've just described. Obviously, you can't back into pace zones from preexisting heart rate zones if you've never established heart rate zones!

There are many pace-based training systems that prescribe individualized target pace zones for runners based on some measure of their current running ability, such as a recent race time. My favorite among them is the one developed by Greg McMillan, which you can find on his Web site at mcmillanrunning.com. To use it, enter a recent race time or a goal time for a race of any distance between 800 meters and a marathon (or just use an estimate of the time you would run for a race of a certain distance today) and press SUBMIT. The calculator will immediately spit out specific pace targets for every conceivable type of run.

Let's say your most recent race was a 10K, which you completed in 41:33 (6:41 per mile). If you use this performance as your input, McMillan's calculator will recommend that you do your "recovery jogs" at 8:36 to 9:17 per mile, your "easy runs" at 7:31 to 8:31 per mile, your "tempo runs" at 6:41 to 6:58 per mile, your "speed" intervals at distance-specific time ranges of 1:26 to 1:31 for 400 meters up to 6:24 to 6:35 for 1600 meters, and your "sprint" intervals at distance-specific time ranges of 18 to 20 seconds for 100 meters up to 2:03 to 2:12 for 600 meters.

It is not difficult to organize these results in a way that lines up with the perceived effort and heart rate training zones I described earlier in the chapter. Table 6.2 shows how both McMillan's pace guidelines and heart rate–derived pace guidelines line up with heart rate and perceived effort in my five-zone intensity system.

Note that McMillan's pace guidelines for high-intensity intervals are all distance-based, whereas some coaches and training plans use time-based workouts. Most of the workouts you will see in the next chapter, in fact, are time based. To perform time-based high-intensity workouts with Greg McMillan's pace guidelines, you will need to convert his suggested times for intervals of specific distances into a pace in minutes and seconds per mile.

For example, suppose a certain workout features three-minute intervals in Zone 4. According to Table 6.2, Zone 4 intervals are to be performed at McMillan's speed pace for 1000-meter or

TABLE 6.2   **THREE METRIC GUIDELINES FOR THE FIVE INTENSITY ZONES**

	HEART RATE (PERCENT OF LACTATE THRESHOLD)	PERCEIVED EFFORT	PACE
ZONE 1	75–80	1–2	Pace range corresponding to Zone 1 heart rate range OR McMillan Recovery Run Pace
ZONE 2	81–89	3–4	Pace range corresponding to Zone 2 heart rate range OR McMillan Easy/Long Run Pace
ZONE 3	96–100	5.5–6	Pace range corresponding to Zone 3 heart rate range OR McMillan Tempo Run Pace
ZONE 4	102–105	7–8	Pace range corresponding to Zone 4 heart rate range OR McMillan Speed Pace for 1200–1000m Intervals
ZONE 5	106+	9–10	Pace range corresponding to Zone 5 heart rate range OR McMillan Speed/Sprint Pace for 600–100m Intervals

1200-meter intervals. Which of these two options you select should depend on whether you are likely to run closer to 1000 meters or 1200 meters in three minutes at Zone 4 intensity. For most runners, it will be 1000 meters. If this is true for you, find the recommended times for 1000-meter intervals that are associated with the race time you've used as input to McMillan's calculator. Let's go back to our earlier example of a 41:33 10K. The 1000-meter interval time range that corresponds to this race time is 3:48 to 4:01. Now convert these times into mile-based paces. One mile is roughly 1610 meters, so you'll need to inflate these times by 1.61. This calculation yields a target pace range of 6:07 to 6:27 per mile for your three-minute Zone 4 intervals.

TABLE 6.3 **SUMMARY OF INTENSITY MONITORING METRICS**

	ADVANTAGE	DRAWBACK	BEST USE
Perceived Effort	Best indicator of body's current limits and state	Becomes decoupled from actual intensity as fatigue accumulates	Establishing intensity at start of run or run segment Adjusting intensity on "flat" days
Heart Rate	Effective for holding runners back on easy days	Not useful in high-intensity run segments	Establishing custom intensity targets for workouts Monitoring and controlling intensity in low- and moderate-intensity runs and run segments
Pace	Measures intensity in performance terms	Entices runners to push themselves in every run	Monitoring and controlling intensity in moderate- and high-intensity runs and run segments

As your fitness level changes, you will need to recalculate your pace zones—regardless of which method you used to calculate them in the first place—to keep them current. Each time you update your heart rate zones, repeat the process of determining the pace ranges that correspond with these zones. If you use Greg McMillan's pace guidelines, recalculate your pace zones after each race, using your latest finish time as the new input.

Naturally, hills affect the relationship between pace and intensity. A pace of 7:09 per mile on level ground corresponds to a lower intensity than does the same pace on a hill with a 5 percent gradient. Heart rate is a more useful metric for monitoring and controlling intensity on hills because a heart rate of, say, 136 beats per minute represents the same physiological intensity whether you're running uphill, downhill, or on level ground.

Due to cardiac lag, however, heart rate monitoring itself is not helpful when you are running short uphill intervals at high intensity. In this case, it's best to use perceived effort as your primary intensity metric while also paying attention to your time to complete each hill interval. Aim to match or slightly improve those times when you repeat the workout.

COMBINING PERCEIVED EFFORT, HEART RATE, AND PACE

I've given you a lot of information in this chapter. If it all seems overwhelming at this point, relax. My guidelines for monitoring and controlling intensity by perceived effort, heart rate, and pace can be summarized in a few key points. Here they are:

- Start by doing either a thirty-minute time trial, a perceived effort–based test workout, or a talk-test workout to determine your lactate threshold heart rate, then calculate your five heart rate training zones using the percentages in Table 6.1.
- Use one of these same workouts to calibrate your perceived effort ratings, anchoring your lactate threshold intensity to a perceived effort of 6 on a 1 to 10 scale.
- Determine target pace ranges that correspond to your five heart rate zones either by finding the pace that corresponds with the heart rate marking the low end and high end of each zone or by using the McMillan calculator.
- Use perceived effort to establish your initial intensity whenever a workout calls for a change in intensity.
- Use heart rate as your primary intensity metric in all low-intensity runs (Zones 1 and 2).
- Use both heart rate and pace to regulate intensity when running at moderate intensity (Zone 3).
- If you prefer not to train with a heart rate monitor, you may use pace to regulate your intensity whenever you would otherwise use heart rate, basing your target zones on Greg McMillan's pace guidelines, but if you do this, it is imperative that you stay within those zones at all times, especially in low-intensity runs.

- Use pace as your primary intensity metric when running at high intensity (Zones 4 and 5), except when running uphill, in which case you should rely on perceived effort.
- Use perceived effort to fine-tune your intensity during your most challenging workouts. Specifically, use it to ensure you finish all such runs feeling you could have run at least a little faster or farther.
- Use perceived effort to adjust your intensity on "flat" days. Specifically, when you feel worse than normal at a given target heart rate or pace, slow down.

At the back of this book, you will find an Appendix with further instructions for intensity regulation that are specific to each type of workout, from basic recovery runs to multizone mixed interval runs. Treat your first attempt or two at applying these instructions in each workout type as practice. If you forget your Zone 3 pace range or are a little unsure of your perceived effort ratings, chalk it up to experience and move on. You'll get it right on your next try.

GETTING STARTED WITH 80/20 RUNNING

I have a confession to make: The 80/20 Rule is not quite as simple as I've made it out to be. There is some fine print that you need to understand before you can practice 80/20 running effectively.

Here's another confession: The 80/20 Rule is not the only rule you must follow to get the most out of your training. If all you knew about how to train was that you should do 80 percent of your running at low intensity and 20 percent at moderate and high intensities, you would be left with far too much leeway to make all kinds of other mistakes. For example, the 80/20 Rule says nothing about how to structure the different types of runs or about the proper way to sequence workouts to create a progressive training program. The 80/20 Rule alone doesn't suffice to guarantee successful training. Maximizing the results you get from all of the time and energy you invest in your training will require that you practice the 80/20 Rule in conjunction with several other rules that coaches and runners have also learned through many decades of trial and error and that, alongside the 80/20 Rule, are almost universally practiced by elite runners today.

In this chapter, I will explain the nuances of the 80/20 Rule and describe six additional rules that work synergistically with it to make the training process as effective as it can possibly be. Once you understand these rules and how they fit together, you will know everything you need to know to realize your full potential as a runner.

RULE #1: THE 80/20 RULE (THE FINE PRINT)

The basic formula of the 80/20 Rule is this: "Do 80 percent of your training at low intensity and 20 percent at moderate and high intensities." The complete, fine-print-and-all formulation of the same rule is this: "Do *approximately* 80 percent of your training at low intensity and 20 percent at moderate and high intensities, *except* during specific periods of training when it is beneficial to do somewhat more or somewhat less low-intensity training, and *unless* you learn through experience that you benefit from *slightly* greater or *slightly* lesser amounts of low-intensity running, and be sure to *vary* the balance of moderate- and high-intensity training in your program based on the sort of race you're preparing for." That's a mouthful, I know, but as I spell it all out, you will find the underlying concepts easy enough to grasp.

When Stephen Seiler defined and named the 80/20 Rule, he was making an approximation. His research had shown him that elite athletes in several endurance sports did *about* 80 percent of their training at low intensity and *roughly* 20 percent at moderate and high intensities. No athlete, however, maintains a precise 80/20 balance all the time or even tries to. And even if an athlete did aim for such precision, it would be exceedingly difficult to pull off.

What's more, even if an athlete did manage to maintain a precise 80/20 balance, it wouldn't matter much. There is a general understanding among coaches, athletes, and exercise scientists that small variations in training produce no measurable differences in fitness and performance. Training is a bit like diet in this regard. You do not eat the same amount of food every day. There are day-to-day fluctuations of a few dozen calories, sometimes more, in your food intake. Yet your weight holds fairly steady from week to week. Similarly, if the ratio of your training time spent at low intensity and above low intensity averages out to 78/22 or 82/18 instead of 80/20 on the dot over a period of time, your race results will probably be the same in either case. There's no reason to tie yourself in knots trying to aim for perfectly round numbers. What is important is that you avoid ratios that are way off the mark, such as 100/0, 30/70, and the 50/50 ratio that is the norm for recreational runners.

In short, the ideal balance of training intensities is a narrow range rather than a precise ratio. But that range may be slightly different for individual runners. The 80/20 Rule is what Seiler has referred to as a *population optimum*. This means that a training intensity distribution that is very close to 80/20 is best for most, but not all, runners. A few runners respond better if they do a little less or a little more of their training at low intensity. There is no evidence, however, of extreme "outliers" who respond poorly to 80/20 training and much better to either a heavily speed-based program or to an always-slow regimen that lacks any work at higher intensities. So you can't go wrong by following the 80/20 Rule. It's certainly the place to start. As you gain experience, though, you may find that you respond better to a 70/30 ratio or a 90/10 ratio, in which case you'll want to make that your personal rule. But it's more likely that you will find your sweet spot closer to 80/20.

The sweet spot shifts, however, as the training process moves along. The art of sequencing runs of different types into a progressive program that culminates in peak fitness for one or more races is called *periodization*. Most elite runners use a phased approach to periodization, where certain types of workouts tend to be clustered into a particular period for the sake of achieving a specific fitness objective that is appropriate for that time. Some of these objectives may require that a runner do either more or less than 80 percent of his or her running at low intensity.

The training process starts with a base phase. The primary objective of this phase is to gradually increase running mileage to a target level that is appropriate for the individual runner. In this case it is generally best to do more than 80 percent of training at low intensity, because it's both easier and less risky to increase running mileage when faster running is kept to a modicum. It is important to include some faster running in the base phase, though, because it prepares the body for the harder workouts of the peak phase, when the 80/20 Rule goes into effect.

The last part of the training process, which comes after the peak phase, is called the *taper*. The taper period immediately precedes an important race. The objective of this one- to two-week mini-phase is to rest and prime the body for racing. Research and real-world practice have shown that the best way to achieve this objective is to sharply reduce the overall training volume while continuing to do high-intensity workouts. The contribution of low-intensity running to a well-executed taper may therefore be somewhat less than 80 percent.

The proper balance of *moderate*-intensity and *high*-intensity training also varies by circumstance. Stephen Seiler and his fellow researchers have not found consistent enough evidence to proclaim that one particular way of balancing moderate-intensity and high-intensity training is clearly optimal. On the one hand, they have found that elite athletes tend to do more training at high intensity than they do at moderate intensity, and as we saw in chapter 3, some intriguing studies have demonstrated that endurance athletes get great results from a "polarized" training approach where they do 80 percent of their training at low intensity, 20 percent at high intensity, and *none* at moderate intensity. On the other hand, the most impressive results obtained so far in any study of the effects of 80/20 training on runners were seen in runners who did roughly equal amounts of moderate- and high-intensity training. There is also evidence that athletes get more out of moderate-intensity training than they do out of high-intensity training when preparing for longer events.

While the scientists continue to explore these questions, I believe it's best for runners to follow the current best practices of top coaches by balancing moderate-intensity and high-intensity training situationally. For example, if you are training for a 5K, you should probably do more high-intensity training because 5Ks are typically raced at high intensity. But if you're training for a marathon, you should probably do more moderate-intensity running because it is more specific to the actual demands of marathon racing.

RULE #2: TRAIN IN CYCLES

What would happen if you tried to increase your running fitness every week for as long as you possibly could? Assuming you proceeded in a sensible way, increasing your training load very slowly and giving your body regular opportunities to recover, you would make consistent progress for up to twenty-four weeks. Then you would hit a wall. At that point, any further increases in your training load would yield no further gains in fitness and instead would only leave you more and more fatigued. Eventually, if you did not get injured first, you would develop a severe case of chronic fatigue known as overtraining syndrome, and you would be forced to stop running altogether.

The human body is not able to absorb increasing training loads for longer than about twenty-four weeks at a stretch. For this reason, runners need to train in cycles. Each training cycle must be followed by a recuperative period lasting at least a couple of weeks. Despite losing some fitness during such breaks, you will be able to start the next cycle at a higher level of base fitness than you did the last one, and therefore you will also be able to train harder and attain a higher level of peak fitness.

Training cycles may be shorter than twenty-four weeks. The optimal duration is determined by your initial fitness level and by the distance of your peak race. If your peak race is long, such as a marathon, and your initial fitness level is fairly low, you should allow close to twenty-four weeks to prepare. If your peak race is short, such as a 5K, and your initial fitness level is fairly high, you may need as little as six weeks to attain peak fitness for that distance.

RULE #3: RUN MORE (LITTLE BY LITTLE)

The most effective way to improve as a runner, as you already know, is to follow the 80/20 Rule. The second most effective way to improve is to run more. Once you have corrected the intensity balance in your training, consider increasing your running volume. If currently you run only three or four times per week, set a goal to run six or seven times per week. According to the World Health Organization, *daily* aerobic exercise is required for maximum all-around health. As a runner, you might as well meet this requirement by running. Not only will your health improve but your running will too.

Once you're consistently running six or seven times per week, a sensible next step is to increase the average duration of your runs to one hour. When you reach that point, you'll be running a total of six or seven hours per week. You can cover a lot of ground in six or seven hours. If your average pace is ten minutes per mile, you'll run forty-two miles in a seven-hour training week. By running longer one day per week, you can get your total weekly running volume closer to fifty miles.

Take your time building your running volume. The body's tolerance for the stress of running increases slowly. It's best to err on the side of caution and proceed even slower than you think you could. Aim to boost your average weekly running volume by no more than ten miles from year to year. Even at this cautious rate, you can go from twenty miles per week to sixty miles per week in four years.

Each runner has a personal running volume limit, which is usually greater than the runner's current limit. If your ultimate goal is to become the best runner you can possibly be, then you'll want to continue to increase your running volume until your current limit merges with your final genetic limit. This is the point beyond which there is no possibility for further improvement by means of additional running. Typically it takes many years of cautious and consistent development for a runner to reach this limit, which, again, is different for each of us.

Outside of the elite ranks, few runners discover their personal maximum running volume. Running just isn't important enough for most recreational runners to make that kind of commitment. Each runner must decide how much time and effort he's willing to commit toward improvement. I am not going to badger you into running more than you want to, but I would like to persuade you to *want* to run more than you do today. And if I can't do that, then at the very least I would like you to recognize that running more is always available to you as your best option for improvement once you're following the 80/20 Rule. If you don't care to run more now, you can always change your mind at some point in the future.

Besides the matter of willingness, a separate impediment to running more is fear of injury. In chapter 12, I will show you how to work around this issue by using cross-training as an alternative to running more.

RULE #4: DO TRIED-AND-TRUE WORKOUTS

There are several distinct types of runs that are practiced almost universally by elite runners. Like the 80/20 Rule, these workouts emerged as best practices through decades of collective trial and error. Nonelite runners rarely include all of these workouts in their training. Adding any "missing" workout types to your program and practicing each type correctly will help you follow the 80/20 Rule more faithfully and get better results from your training.

I briefly mentioned the various types of runs in chapter 6. I will now describe them in more detail and present a full spectrum of formats for each. You can draw upon these workout "menus" to create 80/20 running plans for yourself. To show you how it's done, I've used these same menus to create the training plans that are offered in chapters 8 through 11. For reasons of space economy, these schedules include only the names of the workouts (e.g., "Long Run 5"), not their full descriptions, so you'll need to refer back to these pages for the details.

There are a dozen types of run in all. They are divided into three categories. Low-intensity runs take place entirely in Zones 1 and 2 (refer back to chapter 6 for zone descriptions). Moderate-intensity runs include at least one segment in Zone 3. High-intensity runs feature multiple efforts in Zone 4 or 5 or both.

The "Intensity Breakdown" information given in the right-hand column of each table will help you balance your training appropriately when you create training programs from these menus. When selecting the workout types and levels to include in a given week, tally up the total time spent at low intensity and the total time spent at all intensities and divide the former by the latter to see how close the result comes to 0.80, or 80 percent. If it's not close enough, make an adjustment.

Note that in the case of interval-type workouts that feature relatively short active recovery periods between high-intensity efforts, the entire interval section of the workout, including recovery periods, is counted as time spent at high intensity. Stephen Seiler has argued that this method best reflects the actual stressfulness and training effect of this type of workout.

Low-Intensity Runs

Recovery runs, foundation runs, and long runs include efforts in Zones 1 and 2 only.

RECOVERY RUNS

A recovery run is a run undertaken entirely in Zone 1. These runs are intended to be done as the next run after a very challenging workout. Often an alternative to taking a day off, they serve to increase running volume in a gentle way that does not interfere with recovery from recent hard training.

NAME	FORMAT	INTENSITY BREAKDOWN
Recovery Run 1 (20:00)	20 minutes in Zone 1	Low intensity: 20 minutes
Recovery Run 2 (25:00)	25 minutes in Zone 1	Low intensity: 25 minutes
Recovery Run 3 (30:00)	30 minutes in Zone 1	Low intensity: 30 minutes
Recovery Run 4 (35:00)	35 minutes in Zone 1	Low intensity: 35 minutes
Recovery Run 5 (40:00)	40 minutes in Zone 1	Low intensity: 40 minutes
Recovery Run 6 (45:00)	45 minutes in Zone 1	Low intensity: 45 minutes
Recovery Run 7 (50:00)	50 minutes in Zone 1	Low intensity: 50 minutes
Recovery Run 8 (55:00)	55 minutes in Zone 1	Low intensity: 55 minutes
Recovery Run 9 (60:00)	60 minutes in Zone 1	Low intensity: 60 minutes

FOUNDATION RUNS

A foundation run is a steady, low-intensity run of short to moderate duration. It begins with a warm-up in Zone 1, then moves to Zone 2 for a while, and concludes with a cool-down back in Zone 1. Foundation runs are the bread and butter of effective 80/20 training—the workout type you'll rely on more than any other to ensure you're doing enough running at low intensity.

NAME	FORMAT	INTENSITY BREAKDOWN
Foundation Run 1 (20:00)	5 minutes in Zone 1 10 minutes in Zone 2 5 minutes in Zone 1	Low intensity: 20 minutes
Foundation Run 2 (25:00)	5 minutes in Zone 1 15 minutes in Zone 2 5 minutes in Zone 1	Low intensity: 25 minutes

(continued)

NAME	FORMAT	INTENSITY BREAKDOWN
Foundation Run 3 (30:00)	5 minutes in Zone 1 20 minutes in Zone 2 5 minutes in Zone 1	Low intensity: 30 minutes
Foundation Run 4 (35:00)	5 minutes in Zone 1 25 minutes in Zone 2 5 minutes in Zone 1	Low intensity: 35 minutes
Foundation Run 5 (40:00)	5 minutes in Zone 1 30 minutes in Zone 2 5 minutes in Zone 1	Low intensity: 40 minutes
Foundation Run 6 (45:00)	5 minutes in Zone 1 35 minutes in Zone 2 5 minutes in Zone 1	Low intensity: 45 minutes
Foundation Run 7 (50:00)	5 minutes in Zone 1 40 minutes in Zone 2 5 minutes in Zone 1	Low intensity: 50 minutes
Foundation Run 8 (55:00)	5 minutes in Zone 1 45 minutes in Zone 2 5 minutes in Zone 1	Low intensity: 55 minutes
Foundation Run 9 (60:00)	5 minutes in Zone 1 50 minutes in Zone 2 5 minutes in Zone 1	Low intensity: 60 minutes

LONG RUNS

A long run is simply an extended foundation run that is measured in distance instead of time. Somewhat arbitrarily, I place the minimum long run distance at six miles. With most workouts, time is a better way to give runners of different abilities an equal challenge. For example, if I tell two runners to run five miles, and one runs ten-minute miles and the other runs six-minute miles, the slower runner is going to be out there for almost an hour while the faster runner is only going to get a half hour of training. It's better to give everyone a time and let the faster runner cover more distance in that time. But long runs are different, because their job is to build the endurance needed to cover a particular race distance. So long runs really need to be prescribed in distance to give every runner equal preparation to go the distance in their race.

NAME	FORMAT	INTENSITY BREAKDOWN
Long Run 1 (6 miles)	1 mile in Zone 1 4.5 miles in Zone 2 0.5 mile in Zone 1	Low intensity: 42–72 minutes depending on pace
Long Run 2 (7 miles)	1 mile in Zone 1 5.5 miles in Zone 2 0.5 mile in Zone 1	Low intensity: 49–84 minutes depending on pace
Long Run 3 (8 miles)	1 mile in Zone 1 6.5 miles in Zone 2 0.5 mile in Zone 1	Low intensity: 56–96 minutes depending on pace
Long Run 4 (9 miles)	1 mile in Zone 1 7.5 miles in Zone 2 0.5 mile in Zone 1	Low intensity: 63–108 minutes depending on pace
Long Run 5 (10 miles)	1 mile in Zone 1 8.5 miles in Zone 2 0.5 mile in Zone 1	Low intensity: 70–120 minutes depending on pace
Long Run 6 (11 miles)	1 mile in Zone 1 9.5 miles in Zone 2 0.5 mile in Zone 1	Low intensity: 77–132 minutes depending on pace
Long Run 7 (12 miles)	1 mile in Zone 1 10.5 miles in Zone 2 0.5 mile in Zone 1	Low intensity: 84–144 minutes depending on pace
Long Run 8 (13 miles)	1 mile in Zone 1 11.5 miles in Zone 2 0.5 mile in Zone 1	Low intensity: 91–156 minutes depending on pace
Long Run 9 (14 miles)	1 mile in Zone 1 12.5 miles in Zone 2 0.5 mile in Zone 1	Low intensity: 98–168 minutes depending on pace
Long Run 10 (15 miles)	1 mile in Zone 1 13.5 miles in Zone 2 0.5 mile in Zone 1	Low intensity: 105–180 minutes depending on pace
Long Run 11 (16 miles)	1 mile in Zone 1 14.5 miles in Zone 2 0.5 mile in Zone 1	Low intensity: 112–192 minutes depending on pace
Long Run 12 (17 miles)	1 mile in Zone 1 15.5 miles in Zone 2 0.5 mile in Zone 1	Low intensity: 119–204 minutes depending on pace
Long Run 13 (18 miles)	1 mile in Zone 1 16.5 miles in Zone 2 0.5 mile in Zone 1	Low intensity: 126–216 minutes depending on pace

(continued)

NAME	FORMAT	INTENSITY BREAKDOWN
Long Run 14 (19 miles)	1 mile in Zone 1 17.5 miles in Zone 2 0.5 mile in Zone 1	Low intensity: 133–228 minutes depending on pace
Long Run 15 (20 miles)	1 mile in Zone 1 18.5 miles in Zone 2 0.5 mile in Zone 1	Low intensity: 140–240 minutes depending on pace

Moderate-Intensity Runs

Fast finish runs, tempo runs, long runs with speed play, and long runs with fast finish include efforts in Zone 3.

FAST FINISH RUNS

A fast finish run tacks a relatively short effort in Zone 3 onto the end of a foundation run. Fast finish runs are particularly useful as a way to infuse a little moderate-intensity running into your training during the base phase, when your focus is on increasing volume, and during recovery weeks, when you may want just a "maintenance dose" of moderate-intensity work.

NAME	FORMAT	INTENSITY BREAKDOWN
Fast Finish Run 1 (25:00)	5 minutes Zone 1 15 minutes Zone 2 5 minutes Zone 3	Low intensity: 20 minutes Moderate intensity: 5 minutes
Fast Finish Run 2 (30:00)	5 minutes Zone 1 20 minutes Zone 2 5 minutes Zone 3	Low intensity: 25 minutes Moderate intensity: 5 minutes
Fast Finish Run 3 (35:00)	5 minutes Zone 1 20 minutes Zone 2 10 minutes Zone 3	Low intensity: 25 minutes Moderate intensity: 10 minutes
Fast Finish Run 4 (40:00)	5 minutes Zone 1 25 minutes Zone 2 10 minutes Zone 3	Low intensity: 30 minutes Moderate intensity: 10 minutes

NAME	FORMAT	INTENSITY BREAKDOWN
Fast Finish Run 5 (42:00)	5 minutes Zone 1 25 minutes Zone 2 12 minutes Zone 3	Low intensity: 30 minutes Moderate intensity: 12 minutes
Fast Finish Run 6 (47:00)	5 minutes Zone 1 30 minutes Zone 2 12 minutes Zone 3	Low intensity: 35 minutes Moderate intensity: 12 minutes
Fast Finish Run 7 (52:00)	5 minutes Zone 1 35 minutes Zone 2 12 minutes Zone 3	Low intensity: 40 minutes Moderate intensity: 12 minutes
Fast Finish Run 8 (55:00)	5 minutes Zone 1 35 minutes Zone 2 15 minutes Zone 3	Low intensity: 40 minutes Moderate intensity: 15 minutes
Fast Finish Run 9 (60:00)	5 minutes Zone 1 40 minutes Zone 2 15 minutes Zone 3	Low intensity: 45 minutes Moderate intensity: 15 minutes
Fast Finish Run 10 (65:00)	5 minutes Zone 1 45 minutes Zone 2 15 minutes Zone 3	Low intensity: 50 minutes Moderate intensity: 15 minutes

TEMPO RUNS

A tempo run is a sustained effort in Zone 3 sandwiched between a warm-up and a cool-down. Tempo runs are a very effective means of enhancing a runner's ability to sustain relatively aggressive speeds. They are emphasized in the peak phase of training for races of all distances from 5K to the marathon.

NAME	FORMAT	INTENSITY BREAKDOWN
Tempo Run 1 (35:00)	5 minutes Zone 1 5 minutes Zone 2 15 minutes Zone 3 5 minutes Zone 2 5 minutes Zone 1	Low intensity: 20 minutes Moderate intensity: 15 minutes
Tempo Run 2 (38:00)	5 minutes Zone 1 5 minutes Zone 2 18 minutes Zone 3 5 minutes Zone 2 5 minutes Zone 1	Low intensity: 20 minutes Moderate intensity: 18 minutes

(continued)

NAME	FORMAT	INTENSITY BREAKDOWN
Tempo Run 3 (40:00)	5 minutes Zone 1 5 minutes Zone 2 20 minutes Zone 3 5 minutes Zone 2 5 minutes Zone 1	Low intensity: 20 minutes Moderate intensity: 20 minutes
Tempo Run 4 (44:00)	5 minutes Zone 1 5 minutes Zone 2 24 minutes Zone 3 5 minutes Zone 2 5 minutes Zone 1	Low intensity: 20 minutes Moderate intensity: 24 minutes
Tempo Run 5 (48:00)	5 minutes Zone 1 5 minutes Zone 2 28 minutes Zone 3 5 minutes Zone 2 5 minutes Zone 1	Low intensity: 20 minutes Moderate intensity: 28 minutes
Tempo Run 6 (50:00)	5 minutes Zone 1 5 minutes Zone 2 30 minutes Zone 3 5 minutes Zone 2 5 minutes Zone 1	Low intensity: 20 minutes Moderate intensity: 30 minutes
Tempo Run 7 (52:00)	5 minutes Zone 1 5 minutes Zone 2 32 minutes Zone 3 5 minutes Zone 2 5 minutes Zone 1	Low intensity: 20 minutes Moderate intensity: 32 minutes
Tempo Run 8 (56:00)	5 minutes Zone 1 5 minutes Zone 2 36 minutes Zone 3 5 minutes Zone 2 5 minutes Zone 1	Low intensity: 20 minutes Moderate intensity: 36 minutes
Tempo Run 9 (60:00)	5 minutes Zone 1 5 minutes Zone 2 40 minutes Zone 3 5 minutes Zone 2 5 minutes Zone 1	Low intensity: 20 minutes Moderate intensity: 40 minutes
Tempo Run 10 (65:00)	5 minutes Zone 1 5 minutes Zone 2 45 minutes Zone 3 5 minutes Zone 2 5 minutes Zone 1	Low intensity: 20 minutes Moderate intensity: 45 minutes

CRUISE INTERVAL RUNS

A cruise interval run features multiple long intervals in Zone 3 separated by Zone 1 recoveries. These runs offer essentially the same benefits as tempo runs, but because the Zone 3 running is divided up, they allow more total work to be done at moderate intensity.

NAME	FORMAT	INTENSITY BREAKDOWN
Cruise Interval Run 1 (52:00)	5 minutes Zone 1 5 minutes Zone 2 4 x (5 minutes Zone 3/3 minutes Zone 1) 5 minutes Zone 2 5 minutes Zone 1	Low intensity: 20 minutes Moderate intensity: 32 minutes
Cruise Interval Run 2 (64:00)	5 minutes Zone 1 5 minutes Zone 2 4 x (8 minutes Zone 3/3 minutes Zone 1) 5 minutes Zone 2 5 minutes Zone 1	Low intensity: 20 minutes Moderate intensity: 44 minutes
Cruise Interval Run 3 (72:00)	5 minutes Zone 1 5 minutes Zone 2 4 x (10 minutes Zone 3/3 minutes Zone 1) 5 minutes Zone 2 5 minutes Zone 1	Low intensity: 20 minutes Moderate intensity: 52 minutes
Cruise Interval Run 4 (80:00)	5 minutes Zone 1 5 minutes Zone 2 4 x (12 minutes Zone 3/3 minutes Zone 1) 5 minutes Zone 2 5 minutes Zone 1	Low intensity: 20 minutes Moderate intensity: 60 minutes
Cruise Interval Run 5 (92:00)	5 minutes Zone 1 5 minutes Zone 2 4 x (15 minutes Zone 3/3 minutes Zone 1) 5 minutes Zone 2 5 minutes Zone 1	Low intensity: 20 minutes Moderate intensity: 72 minutes

LONG RUNS WITH SPEED PLAY

A long run with speed play is an endurance run that's done mostly at low intensity but has short bursts in Zone 3 sprinkled throughout it. Long runs with speed play are good workouts to do late in a training cycle when you've already built the basic endurance you need to achieve your peak race goal (i.e., when you've already done the longest long run you intend to do). The addition of Zone 3 efforts serves to increase fatigue resistance beyond the extent that can be accomplished through long runs done entirely at low intensity. Like other types of long runs, long runs with speed play are measured in distance instead of time.

NAME	FORMAT	INTENSITY BREAKDOWN
Long Run with Speed Play 1 (10 miles)	0.5 mile Zone 1 1 mile Zone 2 8 x (0.25 mile Zone 3/0.75 mile Zone 2) 0.5 mile Zone 1	Low intensity: 56–96 minutes depending on pace Moderate intensity: 12–20 minutes depending on pace
Long Run with Speed Play 2 (12 miles)	0.5 mile Zone 1 1 mile Zone 2 10 x (0.25 mile Zone 3/0.75 mile Zone 2) 0.5 mile Zone 1	Low intensity: 65–111 minutes depending on pace Moderate intensity: 15–25 minutes depending on pace
Long Run with Speed Play 3 (14 miles)	0.5 mile Zone 1 1 mile Zone 2 12 x (0.25 mile Zone 3/0.75 mile Zone 2) 0.5 mile Zone 1	Low intensity: 74–126 minutes depending on pace Moderate intensity: 18–30 minutes depending on pace
Long Run with Speed Play 4 (16 miles)	0.5 mile Zone 1 1 mile Zone 2 14 x (0.25 mile Zone 3/0.75 mile Zone 2) 0.5 mile Zone 1	Low intensity: 83–141 minutes depending on pace Moderate intensity: 21–35 minutes depending on pace
Long Run with Speed Play 5 (18 miles)	0.5 mile Zone 1 1 mile Zone 2 16 x (0.25 mile Zone 3/0.75 mile Zone 2) 0.5 mile Zone 1	Low intensity: 92–156 minutes depending on pace Moderate intensity: 24–40 minutes depending on pace

NAME	FORMAT	INTENSITY BREAKDOWN
Long Run with Speed Play 6 (20 miles)	0.5 mile Zone 1 1 mile zone 2 18 x (0.25 mile Zone 3/0.75 mile Zone 2) 0.5 mile Zone 1	Low intensity: 101–171 minutes depending on pace Moderate intensity: 27–45 minutes depending on pace

LONG RUNS WITH FAST FINISH

A long run with fast finish is an extended run at low intensity with a relatively short effort at moderate intensity tacked onto the end. Like long runs with speed play, long runs with fast finish serve to further increase fatigue resistance toward the end of a training cycle after you've already developed basic endurance to "go the distance" in your next race. These workouts are also measured in distance.

NAME	FORMAT	INTENSITY BREAKDOWN
Long Run with Fast Finish 1 (10 miles)	0.5 mile Zone 1 8.5 miles Zone 2 1 mile Zone 3	Low intensity: 63–90 minutes depending on pace Moderate intensity: 6–9 minutes depending on pace
Long Run with Fast Finish 2 (12 miles)	0.5 mile Zone 1 10.5 miles Zone 2 1 mile Zone 3	Low intensity: 77–110 minutes depending on pace Moderate intensity: 6–9 minutes depending on pace
Long Run with Fast Finish 3 (14 miles)	0.5 mile Zone 1 12 miles Zone 2 1.5 miles Zone 3	Low intensity: 87–125 minutes depending on pace Moderate intensity: 10–17 minutes depending on pace
Long Run with Fast Finish 4 (16 miles)	0.5 mile Zone 1 14 miles Zone 2 1.5 miles Zone 3	Low intensity: 101–145 minutes depending on pace Moderate intensity: 10–17 minutes depending on pace
Long Run with Fast Finish 5 (18 miles)	0.5 mile Zone 1 15.5 miles Zone 2 2 miles Zone 3	Low intensity: 112–160 minutes depending on pace Moderate intensity: 14–18 minutes depending on pace

(continued)

NAME	FORMAT	INTENSITY BREAKDOWN
Long Run with Fast Finish 6 (20 miles)	0.5 mile Zone 1 17.5 miles Zone 2 2 miles Zone 3	Low intensity: 126–180 minutes depending on pace Moderate intensity: 14–18 minutes depending on pace

High-Intensity Runs

Speed play runs, hill repetition runs, and interval runs featuring long, short, and mixed intervals include high-intensity efforts in Zones 4 and 5.

SPEED PLAY RUNS

A speed play run is a cross between a foundation run and an interval run. Like foundation runs, speed play runs are done mostly in Zone 2. But this low-intensity backdrop is punctuated by short bursts at high intensity, as in interval runs. Speed play runs are generally intended to be somewhat easier than interval runs, though, and are traditionally done on trails or roads instead of at the track. They are used most often as a low-key way to include some high-intensity running in the base phase of training, when increasing the overall volume of running is the top priority. They also offer a nice break from interval runs in recovery weeks.

NAME	FORMAT	INTENSITY BREAKDOWN
Speed Play Run 1 (27:00)	5 minutes Zone 1 5 minutes Zone 2 3 x (2 minutes Zone 4/2 minutes Zone 1) 5 minutes Zone 1	Low intensity: 15 minutes High intensity: 12 minutes
Speed Play Run 2 (30:00)	5 minutes Zone 1 5 minutes Zone 2 5 x (1 minute Zone 5/2 minutes Zone 1) 5 minutes Zone 1	Low intensity: 15 minutes High intensity: 15 minutes

NAME	FORMAT	INTENSITY BREAKDOWN
Speed Play Run 3 (31:00)	5 minutes Zone 1 5 minutes Zone 2 4 x (2 minutes Zone 4/2 minutes Zone 1) 5 minutes Zone 1	Low intensity: 15 minutes High intensity: 16 minutes
Speed Play Run 4 (33:00)	5 minutes Zone 1 5 minutes Zone 2 6 x (1 minute Zone 5/2 minutes Zone 1) 5 minutes Zone 1	Low intensity: 15 minutes High intensity: 18 minutes
Speed Play Run 5 (35:00)	5 minutes Zone 1 5 minutes Zone 2 5 x (2 minutes Zone 4/2 minutes Zone 1) 5 minutes Zone 1	Low intensity: 15 minutes High intensity: 20 minutes
Speed Play Run 6 (36:00)	5 minutes Zone 1 5 minutes Zone 2 7 x (1 minute Zone 5/2 minutes Zone 1) 5 minutes Zone 1	Low intensity: 15 minutes High intensity: 21 minutes
Speed Play Run 7 (39:00)	5 minutes Zone 1 5 minutes Zone 2 6 x (2 minutes Zone 4/2 minutes Zone 1) 5 minutes Zone 1	Low intensity: 15 minutes High intensity: 24 minutes
Speed Play Run 8 (39:00)	5 minutes Zone 1 5 minutes Zone 2 8 x (1 minute Zone 5/2 minutes Zone 1) 5 minutes Zone 1	Low intensity: 15 minutes High intensity: 24 minutes
Speed Play Run 9 (42:00)	5 minutes Zone 1 5 minutes Zone 2 9 x (1 minute Zone 5/2 minutes Zone 1) 5 minutes Zone 1	Low intensity: 15 minutes High intensity: 27 minutes

(continued)

NAME	FORMAT	INTENSITY BREAKDOWN
Speed Play Run 10 (43:00)	5 minutes Zone 1 5 minutes Zone 2 7 x (2 minutes Zone 4/2 minutes Zone 1) 5 minutes Zone 1	Low intensity: 15 minutes High intensity: 28 minutes
Speed Play Run 11 (45:00)	5 minutes Zone 1 5 minutes Zone 2 10 x (1 minute Zone 5/2 minutes Zone 1) 5 minutes Zone 1	Low intensity: 15 minutes High intensity: 30 minutes
Speed Play Run 12 (47:00)	5 minutes Zone 1 5 minutes Zone 2 8 x (2 minutes Zone 4/2 minutes Zone 1) 5 minutes Zone 1	Low intensity: 15 minutes High intensity: 32 minutes
Speed Play Run 13 (51:00)	5 minutes Zone 1 5 minutes Zone 2 9 x (2 minutes Zone 4/2 minutes Zone 1) 5 minutes Zone 1	Low intensity: 15 minutes High intensity: 36 minutes
Speed Play Run 14 (51:00)	5 minutes Zone 1 5 minutes Zone 2 12 x (1 minute Zone 5/2 minutes Zone 1) 5 minutes Zone 1	Low intensity: 15 minutes High intensity: 36 minutes

HILL REPETITION RUNS

A hill repetition run is essentially an uphill interval run, featuring short segments of uphill running in Zone 5. Hill repetitions offer many of the same benefits as interval runs (namely, increased aerobic capacity and high-intensity fatigue resistance, as well as improved running economy). But hill repetitions are less stressful on the legs because impact forces are much lower on an upward slope. For this reason, hill repetition runs make a good bridge between base training and peak training.

NAME	FORMAT	INTENSITY BREAKDOWN
Hill Repetition Run 1 (27:00)	5 minutes Zone 1 5 minutes Zone 2 6 x (30 seconds Zone 5 uphill/90 seconds Zone 1) 5 minutes Zone 1	Low intensity: 15 minutes High intensity: 12 minutes
Hill Repetition Run 2 (31:00)	5 minutes Zone 1 5 minutes Zone 2 8 x (30 seconds Zone 5 uphill/90 seconds Zone 1) 5 minutes Zone 1	Low intensity: 15 minutes High intensity: 16 minutes
Hill Repetition Run 3 (33:00)	5 minutes Zone 1 5 minutes Zone 2 6 x (1 minute Zone 5 uphill/2 minutes Zone 1) 5 minutes Zone 1	Low intensity: 15 minutes High intensity: 18 minutes
Hill Repetition Run 4 (35:00)	5 minutes Zone 1 5 minutes Zone 2 10 x (30 seconds Zone 5 uphill/90 seconds Zone 1) 5 minutes Zone 1	Low intensity: 15 minutes High intensity: 20 minutes
Hill Repetition Run 5 (39:00)	5 minutes Zone 1 5 minutes Zone 2 12 x (30 seconds Zone 5 uphill/90 seconds Zone 1) 5 minutes Zone 1	Low intensity: 15 minutes High intensity: 24 minutes
Hill Repetition Run 6 (39:00)	5 minutes Zone 1 5 minutes Zone 2 8 x (1 minute Zone 5 uphill/2 minutes Zone 1) 5 minutes Zone 1	Low intensity: 15 minutes High intensity: 24 minutes
Hill Repetition Run 7 (39:00)	5 minutes Zone 1 5 minutes Zone 2 6 x (1.5 minutes Zone 5 uphill/2.5 minutes Zone 1) 5 minutes Zone 1	Low intensity: 15 minutes High intensity: 24 minutes
Hill Repetition Run 8 (45:00)	5 minutes Zone 1 5 minutes Zone 2 10 x (1 minute Zone 5 uphill/2 minutes Zone 1) 5 minutes Zone 1	Low intensity: 15 minutes High intensity: 30 minutes

(continued)

NAME	FORMAT	INTENSITY BREAKDOWN
Hill Repetition Run 9 (47:00)	5 minutes Zone 1 5 minutes Zone 2 8 x (1.5 minutes Zone 5 uphill/2.5 minutes Zone 1) 5 minutes Zone 1	Low intensity: 15 minutes High intensity: 32 minutes
Hill Repetition Run 10 (51:00)	5 minutes Zone 1 5 minutes Zone 2 12 x (1 minute Zone 5 uphill/2 minutes Zone 1) 5 minutes Zone 1	Low intensity: 15 minutes High intensity: 36 minutes
Hill Repetition Run 11 (55:00)	5 minutes Zone 1 5 minutes Zone 2 10 x (1.5 minutes Zone 5 uphill/2.5 minutes Zone 1) 5 minutes Zone 1	Low intensity: 15 minutes High intensity: 40 minutes
Hill Repetition Run 12 (63:00)	5 minutes Zone 1 5 minutes Zone 2 12 x (1.5 minutes Zone 5 uphill/2.5 minutes Zone 1) 5 minutes Zone 1	Low intensity: 15 minutes High intensity: 48 minutes

SHORT INTERVAL RUNS

A short interval run features repeated efforts of sixty to ninety seconds in Zone 5 separated by jogging recoveries in Zone 1. Short intervals enhance aerobic capacity, high-intensity fatigue resistance, and running economy.

NAME	FORMAT	INTENSITY BREAKDOWN
Short Interval Run 1 (33:00)	5 minutes Zone 1 5 minutes Zone 2 6 x (1 minute Zone 5/2 minutes Zone 1) 5 minutes Zone 1	Low intensity: 15 minutes High intensity: 18 minutes
Short Interval Run 2 (39:00)	5 minutes Zone 1 5 minutes Zone 2 8 x (1 minute Zone 5/2 minutes Zone 1) 5 minutes Zone 1	Low intensity: 15 minutes High intensity: 24 minutes

NAME	FORMAT	INTENSITY BREAKDOWN
Short Interval Run 3 (39:00)	5 minutes Zone 1 5 minutes Zone 2 6 x (1.5 minutes Zone 5/2.5 minutes Zone 1) 5 minutes Zone 1	Low intensity: 15 minutes High intensity: 24 minutes
Short Interval Run 4 (45:00)	5 minutes Zone 1 5 minutes Zone 2 10 x (1 minute Zone 5/2 minutes Zone 1) 5 minutes Zone 1	Low intensity: 15 minutes High intensity: 30 minutes
Short Interval Run 5 (47:00)	5 minutes Zone 1 5 minutes Zone 2 8 x (1.5 minutes Zone 5/2.5 minutes Zone 1) 5 minutes Zone 1	Low intensity: 15 minutes High intensity: 32 minutes
Short Interval Run 6 (51:00)	5 minutes Zone 1 5 minutes Zone 2 12 x (1 minute Zone 5/2 minutes Zone 1) 5 minutes Zone 1	Low intensity: 15 minutes High intensity: 36 minutes
Short Interval Run 7 (55:00)	5 minutes Zone 1 5 minutes Zone 2 10 x (1.5 minutes Zone 5/2.5 minutes Zone 1) 5 minutes Zone 1	Low intensity: 15 minutes High intensity: 40 minutes
Short Interval Run 8 (63:00)	5 minutes Zone 1 5 minutes Zone 2 12 x (1.5 minutes Zone 5/2.5 minutes Zone 1) 5 minutes Zone 1	Low intensity: 15 minutes High intensity: 48 minutes

LONG INTERVAL RUNS

A long interval run features repeated efforts of three to five minutes in Zone 4. Long interval runs maximize high-intensity fatigue resistance.

NAME	FORMAT	INTENSITY BREAKDOWN
Long Interval Run 1 (30:00)	5 minutes Zone 1 5 minutes Zone 2 3 x (3 minutes Zone 4/2 minutes Zone 1) 5 minutes Zone 1	Low intensity: 15 minutes High intensity: 15 minutes
Long Interval Run 2 (35:00)	5 minutes Zone 1 5 minutes Zone 2 4 x (3 minutes Zone 4/2 minutes Zone 1) 5 minutes Zone 1	Low intensity: 15 minutes High intensity: 20 minutes
Long Interval Run 3 (39:00)	5 minutes Zone 1 5 minutes Zone 2 3 x (5 minutes Zone 4/3 minutes Zone 1) 5 minutes Zone 1	Low intensity: 15 minutes High intensity: 24 minutes
Long Interval Run 4 (40:00)	5 minutes Zone 1 5 minutes Zone 2 5 x (3 minutes Zone 4/2 minutes Zone 1) 5 minutes Zone 1	Low intensity: 15 minutes High intensity: 25 minutes
Long Interval Run 5 (45:00)	5 minutes Zone 1 5 minutes Zone 2 6 x (3 minutes Zone 4/2 minutes Zone 1) 5 minutes Zone 1	Low intensity: 15 minutes High intensity: 30 minutes
Long Interval Run 6 (47:00)	5 minutes Zone 1 5 minutes Zone 2 4 x (5 minutes Zone 4/3 minutes Zone 1) 5 minutes Zone 1	Low intensity: 15 minutes High intensity: 32 minutes
Long Interval Run 7 (55:00)	5 minutes Zone 1 5 minutes Zone 2 5 x (5 minutes Zone 4/3 minutes Zone 1) 5 minutes Zone 1	Low intensity: 15 minutes High intensity: 40 minutes
Long Interval Run 8 (63:00)	5 minutes Zone 1 5 minutes Zone 2 6 x (5 minutes Zone 4/3 minutes Zone 1) 5 minutes Zone 1	Low intensity: 15 minutes High intensity: 48 minutes

NAME	FORMAT	INTENSITY BREAKDOWN
Long Interval Run 9 (71:00)	5 minutes Zone 1 5 minutes Zone 2 7 x (5 minutes Zone 4/3 minutes Zone 1) 5 minutes Zone 1	Low intensity: 15 minutes High intensity: 56 minutes
Long Interval Run 10 (79:00)	5 minutes Zone 1 5 minutes Zone 2 8 x (5 minutes Zone 4/3 minutes Zone 1) 5 minutes Zone 1	Low intensity: 15 minutes High intensity: 64 minutes

MIXED INTERVAL RUNS

Mixed interval runs are intended to sharpen runners up for racing after they've already built a solid foundation of fitness. Including efforts in Zones 3, 4, and 5, they serve to maintain the fitness gains that have been accrued through workouts individually focused on each of these zones.

NAME	FORMAT	INTENSITY BREAKDOWN
Mixed Interval Run 1 (36:00)	5 minutes Zone 1 5 minutes Zone 2 1 minute Zone 5 2 minutes Zone 1 3 minutes Zone 4 2 minutes Zone 1 5 minutes Zone 3 2 minutes Zone 1 3 minutes Zone 4 2 minutes Zone 1 1 minute Zone 5 5 minutes Zone 1	Low intensity: 15 minutes Moderate/high intensity: 21 minutes

(continued)

Mixed Interval Run 2 (46:00)	5 minutes Zone 1 5 minutes Zone 2 1.5 minutes Zone 5 2 minutes Zone 1 5 minutes Zone 4 2 minutes Zone 1 10 minutes Zone 3 2 minutes Zone 1 5 minutes Zone 4 2 minutes Zone 1 1.5 minute Zone 5 5 minutes Zone 1	Low intensity: 15 minutes Moderate/high intensity: 31 minutes
Mixed Interval Run 3 (59:00)	5 minutes Zone 1 5 minutes Zone 2 2 x (1 minute Zone 5/ 2 minutes Zone 1) 2 x (3 minutes Zone 4/ 2 minutes Zone 1) 10 minutes Zone 3 2 minutes Zone 1 2 x (3 minutes Zone 4/ 2 minutes Zone 1) 2 x (1 minute Zone 5/2 minutes Zone 1) 5 minutes Zone 1	Low intensity: 15 minutes Moderate/high intensity: 44 minutes
Mixed Interval Run 4 (71:00)	5 minutes Zone 1 5 minutes Zone 2 2 x (1.5 minutes Zone 5/2.5 minutes Zone 1) 2 x (5 minutes Zone 4/2 minutes Zone 1) 10 minutes Zone 3 2 minutes Zone 1 2 x (1.5 minutes Zone 5/2 minutes Zone 1) 2 x (5 minutes Zone 4/2 minutes Zone 1) 5 minutes Zone 1	Low intensity: 15 minutes Moderate/high intensity: 56 minutes

RULE #5: OBEY THE HARD/EASY PRINCIPLE

The so-called "hard-easy principle" was developed by University of Oregon coaches Bill Dellinger and Bill Bowerman. This principle states that the hardest runs in a runner's program should not be bunched together but instead should be separated by lighter workouts. It's another one of those practices that makes so much intuitive sense, it's a wonder anyone had to discover it. In any case, the hard-easy principle is now practiced universally by elite runners, who use it to organize their standard weekly workout schedules.

Also known as microcycles, these recurring seven-day workout schedules typically include three designated hard days, which are buffered on either side by at least one day of lighter training. Two of the three hard days feature moderate-intensity or high-intensity runs while the third is reserved for a longer run, which is done mostly or entirely at low intensity. Below is the microcycle template that I employ most often when coaching runners. It is used in all of the training plans in chapters 9 to 12. Shading indicates a hard day.

MONDAY	TUESDAY	WEDNESDAY	THURSDAY	FRIDAY	SATURDAY	SUNDAY
Easy run or rest	Moderate- or high-intensity run	Easy run	Easy run	Moderate- or high-intensity run	Easy run	Long run

RULE #6: PRACTICE STEP CYCLES

Step cycles take the hard-easy principle to a broader time scale. Also known as mesocycles, step cycles are multiweek training blocks in which the running workload is intentionally varied from week to week. In a step cycle, each week of training is slightly more challenging than the preceding, until the last week of the cycle, when the training load is reduced to promote recovery and prepare the body for another round of harder training.

Typically, these adjustments are achieved by increasing and decreasing overall running volume rather than by fiddling with the balance of intensities. For example, if your hardest week of training in a given step cycle features thirty-eight total miles of running and an 80/20 intensity balance, then the subsequent recovery week should feature, say, thirty-one miles of total running and an 80/20 intensity balance instead of something like thirty-eight total miles and a 90/10 intensity balance.

Three-week and four-week step cycles are practiced most commonly. Four-week cycles typically work well for low-mileage runners who don't build up a lot of fatigue. Three-week cycles are often better for runners who push their limits in training and for older runners, who need more rest. The shorter cycles are the safer option generally because they offer more frequent opportunities to catch up on recovery. All of the training plans in chapters 9 to 12 feature three-week step cycles.

Below are examples of how the overall volume of running might be varied in three-week and four-week step cycles.

3-WEEK STEP CYCLE	4-WEEK STEP CYCLE
Week 1: 20 miles	Week 1: 60 miles
Week 2: 24 miles	Week 2: 64 miles
Week 3: 16 miles	Week 3: 68 miles
	Week 4: 50 miles

RULE #7: TRAIN PROGRESSIVELY

The most important characteristic of a training program is its *direction*. A well-designed training program should move you closer and closer to a state of peak race readiness as it goes along. In other words, it should be *progressive*. One way to make the training process progressive is to make it incrementally harder—that is, to increase the overall training load that it administers step by step. I've said plenty about this method already.

A second way to make the training process progressive is to make your hard workouts more and more race specific. A short race such as a 5K demands a slightly different kind of fitness than does a longer race such as a half marathon. If you want to run your best 5K, the peak phase of your training program needs to culminate in some challenging runs that are done at or near 5K race intensity. Likewise, to run your best half marathon, you need to sharpen up for it with a few workouts that closely simulate the endurance and intensity demands of that specific distance. One of the key objectives of the early part of the peak phase of training is to get your body ready to handle these race-specific workouts by doing workouts that are somewhat less race specific. In turn, this period of training should be preceded by a period of general conditioning, or base training, that is more or less the same for all race distances.

Following are examples of race-specific workouts, preparatory workouts, and general conditioning principles for each of four popular race distances.

	5K	10K	HALF MARATHON	MARATHON
RACE-SPE-CIFIC WORK-OUT EXAMPLE	Long Interval Run 4 (40:00 with 5 x 3:00 in Zone 4)	Tempo Run 3 (40:00 with 20:00 in Zone 3)	Long Run with Speed Play 2 (12 miles with 10 x 0.25 mile in Zone 3)	Long Run with Fast Finish 4 (16 miles with 1.5 miles in Zone 3)
PREPARATORY WORKOUT EXAMPLE	Speed Play Run 5 (35:00 with 5 x 2:00 in Zone 4)		Long Run 7 (12 miles)	
GENERAL CONDITIONING	Gradually increasing volume of running, 85% to 90% low intensity, with "hard" runs primarily taking the form of Long Runs, Speed Play Runs, Fast Finish Runs, and Hill Repetition Runs			

THAT'S ALL THERE IS TO IT

You now know everything you need to know to design and execute your own 80/20 running program. If you're not quite ready to take that step, you may want to begin by following one of the training plans in chapters 8 through 11. You can then use these plans as templates for constructing your own, fully customized plans.

8.

80/20 TRAINING PLANS: 5K

A 5-kilometer race is a high-intensity affair. Whether your 5K time is 30 minutes or 15 minutes, your heart rate is likely to reach Zone 4 or 5 before you're even halfway to the finish line. Does this mean that the majority of your training for a 5K should be done at high intensity? Of course not! The 80/20 Rule applies to training for all race distances.

This is not to say that your training should be exactly the same for every race, however. When you're training for a 5K, the 20 percent share of your total training time that is spent at moderate and high intensity should be apportioned differently from when you're training for longer races. Specifically, there should be more emphasis on high-intensity running and less on moderate intensity. Each of the three training plans in this chapter has this emphasis.

All of the plans are nine weeks long and begin with a three-week base phase that is followed by a five-week peak phase and finally a one-week taper phase. Every third week is a recovery week. These weeks are indicated by shading. Refer back to chapter 6 for information about the five training zones and to chapter 7 for details about each workout. Chapter 12 contains guidelines on cross-training.

The far-right column indicates the percentage of total training time in each week that is to be done at low intensity ("L") and at moderate and high intensities combined ("M/H"). You will notice that the breakdown is usually closer to 90/10 than it is to 80/20 within the base period. This is because the primary objective of the base period is to increase overall training volume, and ramping up on mileage is less stressful when the amount of faster running is kept to a modicum. Also note that the intensity breakdown for the race week at the end of each plan does not include the race itself.

LEVEL 1

This plan is appropriate for beginning runners preparing for their first 5K event and for more experienced runners who need or prefer a relatively low-volume training program for any reason. Before you begin the plan, build your training to the point where you are running at least three times per week and doing aerobic exercise six times per week. The training load starts at 2 hours and 10 minutes in Week 1 and peaks at 3 hours and 52 minutes in Week 8.

	MON	TUE	WED	THU	FRI	SAT	SUN	INTENSITY BALANCE
				BASE PHASE				
1		Foundation Run 1	Cross-Train 20:00	Speed Play Run 1	Cross-Train 20:00	Foundation Run 2	Cross-Train 20:00	L: 91% M/H: 9%
2		Fast Finish Run 1	Foundation Run 2 or Cross-Train	Foundation Run 2 or Cross-Train	Speed Play Run 2	Foundation Run 2 or Cross-Train	Foundation Run 3	L: 87% M/H: 13%
3		Fast Finish Run 1	Foundation Run 2 or Cross-Train	Foundation Run 2 or Cross-Train	Speed Play Run 1	Foundation Run 2 or Cross-Train	Foundation Run 3	L: 89% M/H: 11%

	MON	TUE	WED	THU	FRI	SAT	SUN	INTENSITY BALANCE
PEAK PHASE								
4		Speed Play Run 2	Foundation Run 3 or Cross-Train	Foundation Run 3 or Cross-Train	Hill Repetition Run 1	Recovery Run 3 or Cross-Train	Fast Finish Run 2	L: 82% M/H: 18%
5		Speed Play Run 3	Foundation Run 4 or Cross-Train	Foundation Run 4 or Cross-Train	Hill Repetition Run 2	Recovery Run 4 or Cross-Train	Fast Finish Run 3	L: 79% M/H: 21%
6		Speed Play Run 2	Foundation Run 3 or Cross-Train	Foundation Run 3 or Cross-Train	Hill Repetition Run 1	Recovery Run 3 or Cross-Train	Fast Finish Run 2	L: 82% M/H: 18%
7		Speed Play Run 4	Recovery Run 4 or Cross-Train	Foundation Run 4 or Cross-Train	Long Interval Run 1	Recovery Run 4 or Cross-Train	Fast Finish Run 4	L: 79% M/H: 21%
8		Speed Play Run 5	Recovery Run 5 or Cross-Train	Foundation Run 5 or Cross-Train	Long Interval Run 2	Recovery Run 5 or Cross-Train	Fast Finish Run 5	L: 78% M/H: 22%
TAPER PHASE								
9		Long Interval Run 1	Recovery Run 3 or Cross-Train	Foundation Run 3 or Cross-Train	Speed Play Run 1	Recovery Run 1 or Cross-Train	5K Race	L: 75% M/H: 25%

LEVEL 2

This plan was designed for runners who are ready to take their training load up a notch or two in order to improve their 5K time. Before you begin the plan, build your training to the point where you are running at least three times per week, including some short efforts at moderate and high intensities and some easy runs of at least six miles, and where you are doing aerobic exercise seven times per week. The training load starts at 4 hours and 30 minutes in Week 1 and peaks at about 5 hours and 31 minutes in Week 8.

	MON	TUE	WED	THU	FRI	SAT	SUN	INTENSITY BALANCE
BASE PHASE								
1	Foundation Run 5 or Cross-Train	Speed Play Run 3	Foundation Run 5 or Cross-Train	Foundation Run 5 or Cross-Train	Hill Repetition Run 2	Recovery Run 5 or Cross-Train	Long Run 1	L: 88% M/H: 12%
2	Foundation Run 5 or Cross-Train	Speed Play Run 5	Foundation Run 6 or Cross-Train	Foundation Run 5 or Cross-Train	Hill Repetition Run 4	Recovery Run 5 or Cross-Train	Long Run 2	L: 86% M/H: 14%
3		Speed Play Run 3	Foundation Run 6 or Cross-Train	Foundation Run 5 or Cross-Train	Hill Repetition Run 3	Recovery Run 6 or Cross-Train	Long Run 1	L: 86% M/H: 14%
PEAK PHASE								
4	Foundation Run 6 or Cross-Train	Long Interval Run 1	Recovery Run 6 or Cross-Train	Foundation Run 6 or Cross-Train	Short Interval Run 4	Recovery Run 6 or Cross-Train	Fast Finish Run 7	L: 81% M/H: 19%
5	Recovery Run 6 or Cross-Train	Long Interval Run 2	Recovery Run 6 or Cross-Train	Foundation Run 7 or Cross-Train	Short Interval Run 5	Recovery Run 6 or Cross-Train	Fast Finish Run 8	L: 79% M/H: 21%

	MON	TUE	WED	THU	FRI	SAT	SUN	INTENSITY BALANCE
6		Long Interval Run 1	Recovery Run 5 or Cross-Train	Foundation Run 6 or Cross-Train	Short Interval Run 2	Recovery Run 5 or Cross-Train	Fast Finish Run 6	L: 79% M/H: 21%
7	Recovery Run 6 or Cross-Train	Short Interval Run 3	Recovery Run 6 or Cross-Train	Foundation Run 8 or Cross-Train	Long Interval Run 6	Recovery Run 6 or Cross-Train	Fast Finish Run 9	L: 79% M/H: 21%
8	Recovery Run 6 or Cross-Train	Short Interval Run 2	Recovery Run 6 or Cross-Train	Foundation Run 9 or Cross-Train	Long Interval Run 7	Recovery Run 6 or Cross-Train	Fast Finish Run 10	L: 78% M/H: 22%
				TAPER PHASE				
9		Long Interval Run 2	Recovery Run 4 or Cross-Train	Foundation Run 3 or Cross-Train	Speed Play Run 2	Recovery Run 2 or Cross-Train	5K Race	L: 77% M/H: 23%

LEVEL 3

This plan is a good fit for experienced competitive runners who are prepared to train twice a day some days in pursuit of improved 5K performance. Before you begin the plan, build your training to the point where you are running at least three times per week, including some short efforts at moderate and high intensities and some easy runs of at least seven miles, and where you are doing aerobic exercise at least seven times per week. The training load starts at 5 hours and 35 minutes in Week 1 and peaks at about 8 hours and 16 minutes in Week 7.

	MON	TUE	WED	THU	FRI	SAT	SUN	INTENSITY BALANCE
				BASE PHASE				
1	Foundation Run 6 or Cross-Train	Speed Play Run 5 / Foundation Run 4 or Cross-Train	Foundation Run 6 or Cross-Train	Foundation Run 6 or Cross-Train	Hill Repetition Run 4	Recovery Run 6 or Cross-Train	Long Run 2	L: 88% M/H: 12%
2	Foundation Run 6 or Cross-Train	Speed Play Run 10 / Foundation Run 4 or Cross-Train	Foundation Run 6 or Cross-Train	Foundation Run 6 or Cross-Train / Foundation Run 4 or Cross-Train	Hill Repetition Run 5	Recovery Run 6 or Cross-Train	Long Run 3	L: 87% M/H: 13%
3		Speed Play Run 7 / Foundation Run 6 or Cross-Train	Foundation Run 6 or Cross-Train	Foundation Run 6 or Cross-Train	Hill Repetition Run 3	Recovery Run 6 or Cross-Train	Long Run 2	L: 86% M/H: 14%
				PEAK PHASE				
4	Foundation Run 6 or Cross-Train	Long Interval Run 2 / Recovery Run 5 or Cross-Train	Foundation Run 6 or Cross-Train	Foundation Run 6 or Cross-Train / Foundation Run 5 or Cross-Train	Short Interval Run 7	Recovery Run 6 or Cross-Train / Foundation Run 5 or Cross-Train	Tempo Run 6	L: 79% M/H: 21%

	MON	TUE	WED	THU	FRI	SAT	SUN	INTENSITY BALANCE
5	Recovery Run 6 or Cross-Train	Long Interval Run 4	Foundation Run 6 or Cross-Train	Foundation Run 6 or Cross-Train	Short Interval Run 8	Recovery Run 6 or Cross-Train	Tempo Run 7	L: 78% M/H: 22%
		Recovery Run 6 or Cross-Train		Foundation Run 6 or Cross-Train		Foundation Run 6 or Cross-Train		
6		Long Interval Run 2	Foundation Run 6 or Cross-Train	Foundation Run 6 or Cross-Train	Short Interval Run 5	Recovery Run 6 or Cross-Train	Tempo Run 4	L: 80% M/H: 20%
		Recovery Run 5 or Cross-Train		Foundation Run 5 or Cross-Train		Foundation Run 5 or Cross-Train		
7	Recovery Run 6 or Cross-Train	Short Interval Run 4	Foundation Run 6 or Cross-Train	Foundation Run 6 or Cross-Train	Long Interval Run 9	Recovery Run 6 or Cross-Train	Fast Finish Run 10	L: 81% M/H: 19%
		Recovery Run 6 or Cross-Train		Foundation Run 6 or Cross-Train		Foundation Run 6 or Cross-Train		

(continued)

	MON	TUE	WED	THU	FRI	SAT	SUN	INTENSITY BALANCE
8	Recovery Run 6 or Cross-Train	Short Interval Run 3	Foundation Run 6 or Cross-Train	Foundation Run 6 or Cross-Train	Long Interval Run 8	Recovery Run 6 or Cross-Train	Fast Finish Run 8	L: 79% M/H: 21%
		Recovery Run 5 or Cross-Train		Foundation Run 5 or Cross-Train		Foundation Run 5 or Cross-Train		
				TAPER PHASE				
9		Long Interval Run 4	Recovery Run 5 or Cross-Train	Foundation Run 4 or Cross-Train	Speed Play Run 2	Recovery Run 3	5K Race	L: 77% M/H: 23%

9.

80/20 TRAINING PLANS: 10K

t is not uncommon for elite runners to compete in both the 5000 meters and the 10,000 meters at major events such as the NCCA championships, national and world championships, and the Olympic Games. In fact, it's not unheard-of for a single runner to *win* at both distances in the same competition. The reason this is possible is that optimal fitness for the two events is similar, allowing runners to train for both distances simultaneously. Although the 10,000 meters is twice as long, for fit runners the intensity is not much lower (world-record pace in the men's 10,000m is a scant 9 seconds per mile slower than world-record pace in the 5000m).

The training plans in this chapter reflect the fact that optimal 10K fitness is not much different from optimal 5K fitness. They feature just a little more volume and a little more balance between moderate- and high-intensity training than do the corresponding 5K plans presented in the preceding chapter. Of course, all of them are characterized by obedience to the 80/20 Rule within the peak phase.

The plans are twelve weeks long and begin with a six-week base phase that is followed by a four-week peak phase and finally a two-week taper phase. Every third week is a recovery week. These weeks are indicated by shading. Refer back to chapter 6 for information about the five training zones and to chapter 7 for details about each workout. Chapter 12 contains guidelines on cross-training.

The far-right column indicates the percentage of total training time in each week that is to be done at low intensity ("L") and at moderate and high intensities combined ("M/H"). Note that the intensity breakdown for the race week at the end of each plan does not include the race itself.

LEVEL 1

This plan is appropriate for newer runners preparing for their first 10K event and for more experienced runners who need or prefer a relatively low-volume training program for any reason. Before you begin the plan, build your training to the point where you are running at least three times per week for up to 30 minutes or more and are doing aerobic exercise six times per week. The training load starts at 2 hours and 37 minutes in Week 1 and peaks at 3 hours and 56 minutes in Week 10.

	MON	TUE	WED	THU	FRI	SAT	SUN	INTENSITY BALANCE
				BASE PHASE				
1		Fast Finish Run 1	Foundation Run 2 or Cross-Train	Foundation Run 2 or Cross-Train	Speed Play Run 1	Foundation Run 2 or Cross-Train	Foundation Run 3	L: 89% M/H: 11%
2		Fast Finish Run 2	Foundation Run 3 or Cross-Train	Foundation Run 2 or Cross-Train	Speed Play Run 2	Foundation Run 2 or Cross-Train	Foundation Run 4	L: 89% M/H: 11%

	MON	TUE	WED	THU	FRI	SAT	SUN	INTENSITY BALANCE
3		Fast Finish Run 1	Foundation Run 2 or Cross-Train	Foundation Run 2 or Cross-Train	Speed Play Run 1	Foundation Run 2 or Cross-Train	Foundation Run 3	L: 89% M/H: 11%
4		Fast Finish Run 3	Foundation Run 3 or Cross-Train	Foundation Run 2 or Cross-Train	Hill Repetition Run 1	Recovery Run 3 or Cross-Train	Foundation Run 5	L: 88% M/H: 12%
5		Fast Finish Run 3	Foundation Run 3 or Cross-Train	Foundation Run 3 or Cross-Train	Hill Repetition Run 2	Recovery Run 3 or Cross-Train	Foundation Run 6	L: 88% M/H: 12%
6		Fast Finish Run 2	Foundation Run 2 or Cross-Train	Foundation Run 2 or Cross-Train	Hill Repetition Run 1	Recovery Run 3 or Cross-Train	Foundation Run 5	L: 90% M/H: 10%
				PEAK PHASE				
7		Speed Play Run 3	Foundation Run 3 or Cross-Train	Foundation Run 4 or Cross-Train	Short Interval Run 1	Recovery Run 3 or Cross-Train	Foundation Run 5	L: 80% M/H: 20%
8		Speed Play Run 5	Foundation Run 3 or Cross-Train	Foundation Run 4 or Cross-Train	Short Interval Run 2	Recovery Run 4 or Cross-Train	Foundation Run 6	L: 80% M/H: 20%
9		Long Interval Run 1	Foundation Run 3 or Cross-Train	Foundation Run 4 or Cross-Train	Speed Play Run 2	Recovery Run 3 or Cross-Train	Fast Finish Run 2	L: 81% M/H: 19%

(continued)

	MON	TUE	WED	THU	FRI	SAT	SUN	INTENSITY BALANCE
10		Long Interval Run 2	Foundation Run 4 or Cross-Train	Foundation Run 4 or Cross-Train	Mixed Interval Run 2	Recovery Run 4 or Cross-Train	Foundation Run 7	L: 78% M/H: 22%
				TAPER PHASE				
11		Long Interval Run 4	Foundation Run 4 or Cross-Train	Foundation Run 3 or Cross-Train	Mixed Interval Run 1	Foundation Run 3 or Cross-Train	Foundation Run 6	L: 79% M/H: 21%
12		Speed Play Run 2	Foundation Run 3 or Cross-Train	Foundation Run 2 or Cross-Train	Fast Finish Run 1	Recovery Run 1 or Cross-Train	10K Race	L: 85% M/H: 15%

LEVEL 2

This plan was designed for runners who are ready to take their training load up a notch or two in order to improve their 10K time. Before you begin the plan, build your training to the point where you are running at least three times per week, including some short efforts at moderate and high intensities and some easy runs of at least six miles, and where you are doing aerobic exercise seven times per week. The training load starts at 4 hours and 43 minutes in Week 1 and peaks at about 5 hours and 59 minutes in Week 10.

	MON	TUE	WED	THU	FRI	SAT	SUN	INTENSITY BALANCE
				BASE PHASE				
1	Foundation Run 5 or Cross-Train	Fast Finish Run 4	Foundation Run 5 or Cross-Train	Foundation Run 5 or Cross-Train	Speed Play Run 4	Foundation Run 5 or Cross-Train	Long Run 1	L: 90% M/H: 10%
2	Foundation Run 5 or Cross-Train	Fast Finish Run 5	Foundation Run 6 or Cross-Train	Foundation Run 5 or Cross-Train	Speed Play Run 5	Foundation Run 5 or Cross-Train	Long Run 2	L: 89% M/H: 11%
3		Fast Finish Run 4	Foundation Run 5 or Cross-Train	Foundation Run 6 or Cross-Train	Speed Play Run 4	Foundation Run 5 or Cross-Train	Long Run 1	L: 89% M/H: 11%
4	Foundation Run 5 or Cross-Train	Fast Finish Run 7	Foundation Run 6 or Cross-Train	Foundation Run 5 or Cross-Train	Hill Repetition Run 5	Recovery Run 6 or Cross-Train	Long Run 3	L: 89% M/H: 11%
5	Recovery Run 5 or Cross-Train	Fast Finish Run 8	Foundation Run 6 or Cross-Train	Foundation Run 6 or Cross-Train	Hill Repetition Run 6	Recovery Run 6 or Cross-Train	Long Run 4	L: 89% M/H: 11%
6		Fast Finish Run 5	Foundation Run 6 or Cross-Train	Foundation Run 6 or Cross-Train	Hill Repetition Run 3	Recovery Run 6 or Cross-Train	Long Run 2	L: 89% M/H: 11%

(continued)

	MON	TUE	WED	THU	FRI	SAT	SUN	INTENSITY BALANCE
				PEAK PHASE				
7	Foundation Run 6 or Cross-Train	Speed Play Run 7	Foundation Run 6 or Cross-Train	Foundation Run 6 or Cross-Train	Short Interval Run 4	Recovery Run 6 or Cross-Train	Fast Finish Run 9	L: 79% M/H: 21%
8	Recovery Run 6 or Cross-Train	Speed Play Run 10	Foundation Run 7 or Cross-Train	Foundation Run 6 or Cross-Train	Short Interval Run 5	Recovery Run 7 or Cross-Train	Fast Finish Run 10	L: 78% M/H: 22%
9		Long Interval Run 2	Foundation Run 6 or Cross-Train	Foundation Run 5 or Cross-Train	Speed Play Run 6	Recovery Run 6 or Cross-Train	Fast Finish Run 7	L: 79% M/H: 21%
10	Foundation Run 6 or Cross-Train	Long Interval Run 4	Foundation Run 7 or Cross-Train	Foundation Run 6 or Cross-Train	Mixed Interval Run 3	Recovery Run 7 or Cross-Train	Long Run with Speed Play 1	L: 78% M/H: 22%
				TAPER PHASE				
11	Recovery Run 5 or Cross-Train	Long Interval Run 3	Foundation Run 5 or Cross-Train	Foundation Run 5 or Cross-Train	Mixed Interval Run 1	Foundation Run 4 or Cross-Train	Fast Finish Run 7	L: 79% M/H: 21%
12		Speed Play Run 5	Foundation Run 4 or Cross-Train	Foundation Run 3 or Cross-Train	Fast Finish Run 3	Recovery Run 2 or Cross-Train	10K Race	L: 81% M/H: 19%

LEVEL 3

This plan is a good fit for experienced competitive runners who are prepared to train twice a day some days in pursuit of improved 10K performance. Before you begin the plan, build your training to the point where you are running at least three times per week, including some short efforts at moderate and high intensities and some easy runs of at least seven miles, and where you are doing aerobic exercise at least seven times per week. The training load starts at 5 hours and 39 minutes in Week 1 and peaks at about 8 hours and 41 minutes in Week 10.

	MON	TUE	WED	THU	FRI	SAT	SUN	INTENSITY BALANCE
				BASE PHASE				
1	Foundation Run 6 or Cross-Train	Fast Finish Run 4 / Foundation Run 3 or Cross-Train	Foundation Run 6 or Cross-Train	Foundation Run 6 or Cross-Train	Speed Play Run 6	Foundation Run 6 or Cross-Train	Long Run 2	L: 90% M/H: 10%
2	Foundation Run 6 or Cross-Train	Fast Finish Run 5 / Foundation Run 3 or Cross-Train	Foundation Run 6 or Cross-Train	Foundation Run 6 or Cross-Train / Foundation Run 3 or Cross-Train	Speed Play Run 7	Foundation Run 6 or Cross-Train	Long Run 3	L: 90% M/H: 10%

(continued)

	MON	TUE	WED	THU	FRI	SAT	SUN	INTENSITY BALANCE
3		Fast Finish Run 4	Foundation Run 6 or Cross-Train	Foundation Run 6 or Cross-Train	Speed Play Run 6	Foundation Run 5 or Cross-Train	Long Run 4	L: 90% M/H: 10%
		Foundation Run 5 or Cross-Train						
4	Foundation Run 6 or Cross-Train	Tempo Run 2	Foundation Run 6 or Cross-Train	Foundation Run 6 or Cross-Train	Hill Repetition Run 4	Recovery Run 6 or Cross-Train	Long Run with Fast Finish 1	L: 89% M/H: 11%
		Foundation Run 3 or Cross-Train		Foundation Run 3 or Cross-Train		Foundation Run 3 or Cross-Train		
5	Recovery Run 6 or Cross-Train	Tempo Run 3	Foundation Run 6 or Cross-Train	Foundation Run 6 or Cross-Train	Hill Repetition Run 5	Recovery Run 6 or Cross-Train	Long Run with Fast Finish 2	L: 89% M/H: 11%
		Recovery Run 4 or Cross-Train		Foundation Run 4 or Cross-Train		Foundation Run 4 or Cross-Train		
6		Tempo Run 2	Foundation Run 6 or Cross-Train	Foundation Run 6 or Cross-Train	Hill Repetition Run 3	Recovery Run 6 or Cross-Train	Fast Finish Run 9	L: 87% M/H: 13%
		Recovery Run 4 or Cross-Train		Foundation Run 4 or Cross-Train		Foundation Run 4 or Cross-Train		

	MON	TUE	WED	THU	FRI	SAT	SUN	INTENSITY BALANCE
				PEAK PHASE				
7	Foundation Run 6 or Cross-Train	Speed Play Run 10	Foundation Run 6 or Cross-Train	Foundation Run 6 or Cross-Train	Short Interval Run 7	Recovery Run 6 or Cross-Train	Long Run with Speed Play 1	L: 81% M/H: 19%
		Recovery Run 5 or Cross-Train		Foundation Run 5 or Cross-Train		Foundation Run 5 or Cross-Train		
8	Recovery Run 6 or Cross-Train	Speed Play Run 12	Foundation Run 6 or Cross-Train	Foundation Run 6 or Cross-Train	Short Interval Run 8	Recovery Run 6 or Cross-Train	Long Run with Speed Play 2	L: 81% M/H: 19%
		Recovery Run 6 or Cross-Train		Foundation Run 6 or Cross-Train		Foundation Run 6 or Cross-Train		
9		Long Interval Run 4	Foundation Run 5 or Cross-Train	Foundation Run 5 or Cross-Train	Speed Play Run 8	Recovery Run 5 or Cross-Train	Fast Finish Run 10	L: 83% M/H: 17%
		Recovery Run 5 or Cross-Train		Foundation Run 5 or Cross-Train		Foundation Run 5 or Cross-Train		

(continued)

	MON	TUE	WED	THU	FRI	SAT	SUN	INTENSITY BALANCE
10	Foundation Run 6 or Cross-Train	Long Interval Run 7	Foundation Run 6 or Cross-Train	Foundation Run 6 or Cross-Train	Mixed Interval Run 4	Recovery Run 6 or Cross-Train	Long Run with Speed Play 2	L: 81% M/H: 19%
		Recovery Run 6 or Cross-Train		Foundation Run 6 or Cross-Train		Foundation Run 6 or Cross-Train		
TAPER PHASE								
11	Recovery Run 5 or Cross-Train	Long Interval Run 5	Foundation Run 5 or Cross-Train	Foundation Run 5 or Cross-Train	Mixed Interval Run 3	Foundation Run 9 or Cross-Train	Long Run with Speed Play 1	L: 82% M/H: 18%
		Recovery Run 5 or Cross-Train		Foundation Run 5 or Cross-Train				
12		Speed Play Run 5	Foundation Run 4 or Cross-Train	Foundation Run 3 or Cross-Train	Fast Finish Run 3	Recovery Run 2 or Cross-Train	10K Race	L: 81% M/H: 19%

10.

80/20 TRAINING PLANS: HALF MARATHON

Perhaps more than any other event, the half marathon requires well-rounded running fitness. No person can comfortably run 13.1 miles by virtue of a generally "active lifestyle." A focused program of endurance building is required to run that far. Yet a half marathon is not so far that you can't also run it pretty fast if you work on developing high-intensity fatigue resistance alongside raw endurance. The training plans in this chapter were designed to deliver the kind of well-rounded running fitness that is needed for success in the half marathon.

Each of the three plans is fifteen weeks long and begins with a six-week base phase. The Level 1 plan also includes an eight-week peak phase and a one-week taper phase. The Level 2 and Level 3 plans have a seven-week peak phase and a two-week taper phase. Every third week is a recovery week. These weeks are indicated by shading. Refer back to chapter 6 for information about the five training zones and to chapter 7 for details about each workout. Chapter 12 contains guidelines on cross-training.

The far-right column indicates the percentage of total training time in each week that is to be done at low intensity ("L") and at moderate and high intensities combined ("M/H"). Note that the intensity breakdown for the race week at the end of each plan does not include the race itself.

LEVEL 1

This plan is appropriate for newer runners preparing for their first half marathon and for more experienced runners who need or prefer a relatively low-volume training program for any reason. Before you begin the plan, build your training to the point where you are running at least three times per week for up to 6 miles or more and are doing aerobic exercise six times per week. The training load starts at 3 hours and 9 minutes in Week 1 and peaks at 4 hours and 56 minutes in Week 14.

	MON	TUE	WED	THU	FRI	SAT	SUN	INTENSITY BALANCE
					BASE PHASE			
1		Fast Finish Run 1	Foundation Run 2 or Cross-Train	Foundation Run 2 or Cross-Train	Speed Play Run 2	Foundation Run 2 or Cross-Train	Long Run 1	L: 89% M/H: 11%
2		Fast Finish Run 2	Foundation Run 3 or Cross-Train	Foundation Run 2 or Cross-Train	Speed Play Run 1	Foundation Run 2 or Cross-Train	Long Run 2	L: 91% M/H: 9%
3		Fast Finish Run 1	Foundation Run 2 or Cross-Train	Foundation Run 2 or Cross-Train	Speed Play Run 2	Foundation Run 2 or Cross-Train	Long Run 1	L: 89% M/H: 11%
4		Fast Finish Run 3	Foundation Run 3 or Cross-Train	Foundation Run 2 or Cross-Train	Hill Reps Run 2	Recovery Run 3 or Cross-Train	Long Run 3	L: 88% M/H: 12%

	MON	TUE	WED	THU	FRI	SAT	SUN	INTENSITY BALANCE
5		Fast Finish Run 4	Foundation Run 3 or Cross-Train	Foundation Run 3 or Cross-Train	Hill Reps Run 4	Recovery Run 3 or Cross-Train	Long Run 4	L: 88% M/H: 12%
6		Fast Finish Run 2	Foundation Run 2 or Cross-Train	Foundation Run 3 or Cross-Train	Hill Reps Run 3	Recovery Run 3 or Cross-Train	Long Run 2	L: 89% M/H: 11%
PEAK PHASE								
7		Tempo Run 1	Recovery Run 3 or Cross-Train	Foundation Run 4 or Cross-Train	Short Interval Run 2	Recovery Run 3 or Cross-Train	Long Run 5	L: 86% M/H: 14%
8		Cruise Interval Run 1	Recovery Run 4 or Cross-Train	Foundation Run 4 or Cross-Train	Short Interval Run 3	Recovery Run 3 or Cross-Train	Long Run 6	L: 81% M/H: 19%
9		Tempo Run 1	Recovery Run 3 or Cross-Train	Foundation Run 3 or Cross-Train	Short Interval Run 2	Recovery Run 3 or Cross-Train	Long Run 3	L: 83% M/H: 17%
10		Tempo Run 3	Recovery Run 4 or Cross-Train	Foundation Run 4 or Cross-Train	Long Interval Run 2	Recovery Run 4 or Cross-Train	Long Run with Speed Play 1	L: 80% M/H: 20%
11		Tempo Run 4	Recovery Run 4 or Cross-Train	Foundation Run 5 or Cross-Train	Long Interval Run 4	Recovery Run 4 or Cross-Train	Long Run with Fast Finish 1	L: 80% M/H: 20%

(continued)

	MON	TUE	WED	THU	FRI	SAT	SUN	INTENSITY BALANCE
12		Tempo Run 2	Recovery Run 4 or Cross-Train	Foundation Run 4 or Cross-Train	Long Interval Run 3	Recovery Run 4 or Cross-Train	Long Run 3	L: 83% M/H: 17%
13		Tempo Run 5	Recovery Run 4 or Cross-Train	Foundation Run 5 or Cross-Train	Mixed Interval Run 1	Recovery Run 5 or Cross-Train	Long Run with Fast Finish 2	L: 81% M/H: 19%
14		Tempo Run 6	Recovery Run 5 or Cross-Train	Foundation Run 5 or Cross-Train	Mixed Interval Run 1	Recovery Run 5 or Cross-Train	Long Run with Fast Finish 1	L: 80% M/H: 20%
TAPER PHASE								
15		Fast Finish Run 3	Foundation Run 3 or Cross-Train	Foundation Run 2 or Cross-Train	Speed Play Run 1	Recovery Run 1	Half Marathon	L: 84% M/H: 16%

LEVEL 2

This plan was designed for runners who are ready to take their training load up a notch or two in order to improve their half marathon time. Before you begin the plan, build your training to the point where you are running at least three times per week, including some short efforts at moderate and high intensities and some easy runs of at least seven miles, and where you are doing aerobic exercise seven times per week. The training load starts at 4 hours and 44 minutes in Week 1 and peaks at about 6 hours and 20 minutes in Week 13.

	MON	TUE	WED	THU	FRI	SAT	SUN	INTENSITY BALANCE
				BASE PHASE				
1	Foundation Run 5 or Cross-Train	Fast Finish Run 3	Foundation Run 5 or Cross-Train	Foundation Run 5 or Cross-Train	Speed Play Run 4	Foundation Run 5 or Cross-Train	Long Run 2	L: 90% M/H: 10%
2	Foundation Run 5 or Cross-Train	Fast Finish Run 4	Foundation Run 6 or Cross-Train	Foundation Run 5 or Cross-Train	Speed Play Run 5	Foundation Run 5 or Cross-Train	Long Run 3	L: 90% M/H: 10%
3		Fast Finish Run 3	Foundation Run 5 or Cross-Train	Foundation Run 5 or Cross-Train	Speed Play Run 4	Foundation Run 5 or Cross-Train	Long Run 1	L: 88% M/H: 12%
4	Foundation Run 5 or Cross-Train	Fast Finish Run 4	Recovery Run 6 or Cross-Train	Foundation Run 6 or Cross-Train	Hill Repetition Run 5	Recovery Run 5 or Cross-Train	Long Run 5	L: 90% M/H: 10%
5	Foundation Run 5 or Cross-Train	Fast Finish Run 5	Recovery Run 6 or Cross-Train	Foundation Run 6 or Cross-Train	Hill Repetition Run 6	Recovery Run 6 or Cross-Train	Long Run 7	L: 90% M/H: 10%
6		Fast Finish Run 4	Recovery Run 5 or Cross-Train	Foundation Run 5 or Cross-Train	Hill Repetition Run 4	Recovery Run 5 or Cross-Train	Long Run 3	L: 88% M/H: 12%
				PEAK PHASE				
7	Foundation Run 6 or Cross-Train	Cruise Interval Run 1	Recovery Run 6 or Cross-Train	Foundation Run 6 or Cross-Train	Short Interval Run 4	Recovery Run 6 or Cross-Train	Long Run with Speed Play 1	L: 79% M/H: 21%

(continued)

	MON	TUE	WED	THU	FRI	SAT	SUN	INTENSITY BALANCE
8	Recovery Run 6 or Cross-Train	Tempo Run 4	Recovery Run 6 or Cross-Train	Foundation Run 6 or Cross-Train	Short Interval Run 5	Recovery Run 6 or Cross-Train	Long Run with Speed Play 2	L: 80% M/H: 20%
9		Cruise Interval Run 1	Recovery Run 5 or Cross-Train	Foundation Run 6 or Cross-Train	Short Interval Run 3	Recovery Run 5 or Cross-Train	Long Run with Fast Finish 1	L: 81% M/H: 19%
10	Foundation Run 6 or Cross-Train	Tempo Run 5	Recovery Run 6 or Cross-Train	Foundation Run 6 or Cross-Train	Long Interval Run 3	Recovery Run 6 or Cross-Train	Long Run with Speed Play 2	L: 81% M/H: 19%
11	Recovery Run 6 or Cross-Train	Cruise Interval Run 2	Recovery Run 6 or Cross-Train	Foundation Run 6 or Cross-Train	Long Interval Run 6	Recovery Run 6 or Cross-Train	Long Run with Fast Finish 2	L: 81% M/H: 19%
12		Tempo Run 4	Recovery Run 5 or Cross-Train	Foundation Run 6 or Cross-Train	Long Interval Run 3	Recovery Run 5 or Cross-Train	Long Run with Speed Play 1	L: 79% M/H: 21%
13	Foundation Run 6 or Cross-Train	Tempo Run 7	Recovery Run 6 or Cross-Train	Foundation Run 6 or Cross-Train	Mixed Interval Run 2	Recovery Run 6 or Cross-Train	Long Run with Fast Finish 3	L: 81% M/H: 19%
				TAPER PHASE				
14	Recovery Run 5 or Cross-Train	Tempo Run 5	Recovery Run 5 or Cross-Train	Foundation Run 4 or Cross-Train	Mixed Interval Run 2	Recovery Run 4 or Cross-Train	Long Run with Speed Play 1	L: 78% M/H: 22%

	MON	TUE	WED	THU	FRI	SAT	SUN	INTENSITY BALANCE
15		Fast Finish Run 5	Foundation Run 4 or Cross-Train	Foundation Run 3 or Cross-Train	Speed Play Run 2	Recovery Run 2	Half Marathon	L: 83% M/H: 17%

LEVEL 3

This plan is a good fit for experienced competitive runners who are prepared to train twice a day some days in pursuit of improved half marathon performance. Before you begin the plan, build your training to the point where you are running at least three times per week, including some short efforts at moderate and high intensities and some easy runs of at least eight miles, and where you are doing aerobic exercise at least seven times per week. The training load starts at 5 hours and 52 minutes in Week 1 and peaks at about 9 hours and 31 minutes in Week 13.

	MON	TUE	WED	THU	FRI	SAT	SUN	INTENSITY BALANCE
				BASE PHASE				
1	Foundation Run 6 or Cross-Train	Fast Finish Run 6 / Foundation Run 3 or Cross-Train	Foundation Run 6 or Cross-Train	Foundation Run 6 or Cross-Train	Speed Play Run 8	Foundation Run 6 or Cross-Train	Long Run 3	L: 90% M/H: 10%

(continued)

	MON	TUE	WED	THU	FRI	SAT	SUN	INTENSITY BALANCE
2	Foundation Run 6 or Cross-Train	Fast Finish Run 7 Foundation Run 3 or Cross-Train	Foundation Run 7 or Cross-Train	Foundation Run 6 or Cross-Train Foundation Run 3 or Cross-Train	Speed Play Run 10	Foundation Run 6 or Cross-Train	Long Run 5	L: 91% M/H: 9%
3		Fast Finish Run 6 Foundation Run 3 or Cross-Train	Foundation Run 6 or Cross-Train	Foundation Run 6 or Cross-Train	Speed Play Run 8	Foundation Run 6 or Cross-Train	Long Run 3	L: 88% M/H: 12%
4	Foundation Run 6 or Cross-Train	Fast Finish Run 8 Foundation Run 4 or Cross-Train	Foundation Run 8 or Cross-Train	Foundation Run 6 or Cross-Train Foundation Run 4 or Cross-Train	Hill Reps Run 7	Recovery Run 6 or Cross-Train Foundation Run 4 or Cross-Train	Long Run 7	L: 91% M/H: 9%
5	Foundation Run 6 or Cross-Train	Fast Finish Run 9 Foundation Run 5 or Cross-Train	Foundation Run 8 or Cross-Train	Foundation Run 6 or Cross-Train Foundation Run 4 or Cross-Train	Hill Reps Run 8	Recovery Run 6 or Cross-Train Foundation Run 4 or Cross-Train	Long Run 9	L: 91% M/H: 9%

	MON	TUE	WED	THU	FRI	SAT	SUN	INTENSITY BALANCE
6		Fast Finish Run 7	Foundation Run 6 or Cross-Train	Foundation Run 6 or Cross-Train	Hill Reps Run 6	Recovery Run 6 or Cross-Train	Long Run 4	L: 90% M/H: 10%
		Foundation Run 4 or Cross-Train		Foundation Run 4 or Cross-Train		Foundation Run 4 or Cross-Train		
PEAK PHASE								
7	Foundation Run 6 or Cross-Train	Cruise Interval Run 2	Foundation Run 9 or Cross-Train	Foundation Run 6 or Cross-Train	Short Interval Run 6	Recovery Run 6 or Cross-Train	Long Run with Speed Play 1	L: 80% M/H: 20%
		Foundation Run 5 or Cross-Train		Foundation Run 5 or Cross-Train		Foundation Run 5 or Cross-Train		
8	Foundation Run 6 or Cross-Train	Tempo Run 6	Foundation Run 9 or Cross-Train	Foundation Run 6 or Cross-Train	Short Interval Run 7	Recovery Run 6 or Cross-Train	Long Run with Speed Play 2	L: 82% M/H: 18%
		Foundation Run 6 or Cross-Train		Foundation Run 6 or Cross-Train		Foundation Run 6 or Cross-Train		

(continued)

	MON	TUE	WED	THU	FRI	SAT	SUN	INTENSITY BALANCE
9		Cruise Interval Run 1	Foundation Run 6 or Cross-Train	Foundation Run 5 or Cross-Train	Short Interval Run 4	Recovery Run 5 or Cross-Train	Long Run with Speed Play 1	L: 81% M/H: 19%
		Foundation Run 5 or Cross-Train		Foundation Run 5 or Cross-Train		Foundation Run 5 or Cross-Train		
10	Foundation Run 6 or Cross-Train	Tempo Run 8	Foundation Run 9 or Cross-Train	Foundation Run 6 or Cross-Train	Long Interval Run 7	Recovery Run 6 or Cross-Train	Long Run with Speed Play 3	L: 81% M/H: 19%
		Recovery Run 6 or Cross-Train		Recovery Run 6 or Cross-Train		Recovery Run 6 or Cross-Train		
11	Recovery Run 6 or Cross-Train	Cruise Interval Run 3	Foundation Run 9 or Cross-Train	Foundation Run 6 or Cross-Train	Long Interval Run 8	Recovery Run 6 or Cross-Train	Long Run with Speed Play 3	L: 81% M/H: 19%
		Recovery Run 6 or Cross-Train		Recovery Run 6 or Cross-Train		Recovery Run 6 or Cross-Train		

	MON	TUE	WED	THU	FRI	SAT	SUN	INTENSITY BALANCE
12		Cruise Interval Run 2	Foundation Run 6 or Cross-Train	Foundation Run 5 or Cross-Train	Long Interval Run 3	Recovery Run 5 or Cross-Train	Long Run with Fast Finish 1	L: 81% M/H: 19%
		Recovery Run 5 or Cross-Train		Recovery Run 5 or Cross-Train		Recovery Run 5 or Cross-Train		
13	Recovery Run 6 or Cross-Train	Tempo Run 9	Foundation Run 9 or Cross-Train	Foundation Run 6 or Cross-Train	Mixed Interval Run 4	Recovery Run 6 or Cross-Train	Long Run with Fast Finish 4	L: 80% M/H: 20%
		Recovery Run 6 or Cross-Train		Recovery Run 6 or Cross-Train		Recovery Run 6 or Cross-Train		
TAPER PHASE								
14	Recovery Run 5 or Cross-Train	Tempo Run 6	Foundation Run 5 or Cross-Train	Foundation Run 5 or Cross-Train	Mixed Interval Run 2	Recovery Run 4 or Cross-Train	Long Run with Speed Play 1	L: 83% M/H: 17%
		Recovery Run 5 or Cross-Train		Recovery Run 4 or Cross-Train		Recovery Run 4 or Cross-Train		
15		Fast Finish Run 6	Foundation Run 5 or Cross-Train	Foundation Run 4 or Cross-Train	Speed Play Run 5	Recovery Run 2	Half Marathon	L: 80% M/H: 20%

11.

80/20 TRAINING PLANS: MARATHON

The marathon distance is, in my opinion, a bit longer than humans were meant to race on foot. This is proven by the fact that about 75 percent of the participants in any given marathon, including elite runners, hit the wall in the last several miles and slow down precipitously. The corresponding number in half marathons is only 8 percent. To avoid hitting the wall in your next marathon, you need to build a very high level of endurance and cultivate the ability to run hard in a state of fatigue without slowing down. The training plans in this chapter were designed to minimize your chances of losing momentum after mile 20.

All three plans are eighteen weeks long and begin with a nine-week base phase that is followed by a seven-week peak phase and finally a two-week taper phase. Every third week is a recovery week. These weeks are indicated by shading. Refer back to chapter 6 for information about the five training zones and to chapter 7 for details about each workout. Chapter 12 contains guidelines on cross-training.

The far-right column indicates the percentage of total training time in each week that is to be done at low intensity ("L") and at moderate and high intensities combined ("M/H"). Note that the intensity breakdown for the race week at the end of each plan does not include the race itself.

LEVEL 1

This plan is appropriate for newer runners preparing for their first marathon and for more experienced runners who need or prefer a relatively low-volume training program for any reason. Before you begin the plan, build your training to the point where you are running at least three times per week for up to 6 miles or more and are doing aerobic exercise six times per week. The training load starts at 3 hours and 21 minutes in Week 1 and peaks at 6 hours and 34 minutes in Week 16.

	MON	TUE	WED	THU	FRI	SAT	SUN	INTENSITY BALANCE
				BASE PHASE				
1		Fast Finish Run 2	Foundation Run 3	Foundation Run 3	Speed Play Run 1	Foundation Run 3	Long Run 1	L: 92% M/H: 8%
2		Fast Finish Run 3	Foundation Run 4	Foundation Run 3	Speed Play Run 2	Foundation Run 3	Long Run 2	L: 91% M/H: 9%
3		Fast Finish Run 2	Foundation Run 3	Foundation Run 3	Speed Play Run 1	Foundation Run 3	Long Run 1	L: 92% M/H: 8%
4		Fast Finish Run 4	Foundation Run 4	Foundation Run 3	Hill Repetition Run 1	Recovery Run 4	Long Run 3	L: 91% M/H: 9%
5		Fast Finish Run 6	Foundation Run 4	Foundation Run 4	Hill Repetition Run 2	Recovery Run 4	Long Run 4	L: 90% M/H: 10%
6		Fast Finish Run 4	Foundation Run 3	Foundation Run 4	Hill Repetition Run 1	Recovery Run 3	Long Run 2	L: 90% M/H: 10%
7		Fast Finish Run 7	Foundation Run 5	Foundation Run 4	Hill Repetition Run 4	Recovery Run 4	Long Run 5	L: 89% M/H: 11%

	MON	TUE	WED	THU	FRI	SAT	SUN	INTENSITY BALANCE
8		Fast Finish Run 8	Foundation Run 5	Foundation Run 5	Hill Repetition Run 6	Recovery Run 4	Long Run 7	L: 89% M/H: 11%
9		Fast Finish Run 6	Foundation Run 4	Foundation Run 4	Hill Repetition Run 4	Recovery Run 4	Long Run 4	L: 89% M/H: 11%
				PEAK PHASE				
10		Tempo Run 2	Recovery Run 5	Foundation Run 5	Short Interval Run 1	Recovery Run 4	Long Run 9	L: 88% M/H: 12%
11		Cruise Intervals 1 Run	Recovery Run 5	Foundation Run 5	Short Interval Run 2	Recovery Run 5	Long Run 11	L: 84% M/H: 16%
12		Tempo Run 2	Recovery Run 4	Foundation Run 5	Short Interval Run 1	Recovery Run 4	Long Run with Speed Play 1	L: 79% M/H: 21%
13		Tempo Run 3	Recovery Run 5	Foundation Run 6	Long Interval Run 2	Recovery Run 5	Long Run with Fast Finish 1	L: 83% M/H: 17%
14		Tempo Run 4	Recovery Run 6	Foundation Run 6	Long Interval Run 3	Recovery Run 5	Long Run with Speed Play 2	L: 78% M/H: 22%
15		Tempo Run 2	Recovery Run 5	Foundation Run 5	Long Interval Run 1	Recovery Run 5	Marathon Simulator Run	L: 79% M/H: 21%
16		Cruise Intervals Run 2	Recovery Run 6	Foundation Run 6	Mixed Interval Run 1	Recovery Run 6	Long Run with Fast Finish 5	L: 79% M/H: 81%

(continued)

		MON	TUE	WED	THU	FRI	SAT	SUN	
TAPER PHASE									
17		Tempo Run 4	Foundation Run 5	Foundation Run 5	Mixed Interval Run 1	Recovery Run 4	Long Run with Speed Play 2		L: 79% M/H: 21%
18		Fast Finish Run 4	Foundation Run 4	Foundation Run 3	Speed Play Run 2	Recovery Run 1	Marathon		L: 84% M/H: 16%

LEVEL 2

This plan was designed for runners who are ready to take their training load up a notch or two in order to improve their marathon time. Before you begin the plan, build your training to the point where you are running at least three times per week, including some short efforts at moderate and high intensities and some easy runs of at least eight miles and where you are doing aerobic exercise seven times per week. The training load starts at 4 hours and 52 minutes in Week 1 and peaks at about 6 hours and 56 minutes in Week 13.

	MON	TUE	WED	THU	FRI	SAT	SUN	INTENSITY BALANCE
BASE PHASE								
1	Foundation Run 5 or Cross-Train	Fast Finish Run 4	Foundation Run 5 or Cross-Train	Foundation Run 5 or Cross-Train	Speed Play Run 4	Foundation Run 5 or Cross-Train	Long Run 3	L: 91% M/H: 9%
2	Foundation Run 5 or Cross-Train	Fast Finish Run 6	Foundation Run 5 or Cross-Train	Foundation Run 5 or Cross-Train	Speed Play Run 5	Foundation Run 5 or Cross-Train	Long Run 4	L: 90% M/H: 10%

	MON	TUE	WED	THU	FRI	SAT	SUN	INTENSITY BALANCE
3		Fast Finish Run 4	Foundation Run 5 or Cross-Train	Foundation Run 4 or Cross-Train	Speed Play Run 4	Foundation Run 5 or Cross-Train	Long Run 2	L: 89% M/H: 11%
4	Foundation Run 5 Cross-Train	Fast Finish Run 6	Foundation Run 5 or Cross-Train	Foundation Run 5 or Cross-Train	Hill Repetition Run 4	Recovery Run 5 or Cross-Train	Long Run 5	L: 90% M/H: 10%
5	Foundation Run 5 or Cross-Train	Fast Finish Run 7	Foundation Run 6 or Cross-Train	Foundation Run 5 or Cross-Train	Hill Repetition Run 5	Recovery Run 5 or Cross-Train	Long Run 7	L: 90% M/H: 10%
6		Fast Finish Run 6	Foundation Run 5 or Cross-Train	Foundation Run 5 or Cross-Train	Hill Repetition Run 4	Recovery Run 5 or Cross-Train	Long Run 3	L: 89% M/H: 11%
7	Foundation Run 5 Cross-Train	Fast Finish Run 8	Foundation Run 6 or Cross-Train	Foundation Run 5 or Cross-Train	Hill Repetition Run 6	Recovery Run 6 or Cross-Train	Long Run 9	L: 90% M/H: 10%
8	Foundation Run 5 or Cross-Train	Fast Finish Run 9	Foundation Run 6 or Cross-Train	Foundation Run 6 or Cross-Train	Hill Repetition Run 8	Recovery Run 6 or Cross-Train	Long Run 11	L: 88% M/H: 12%
9		Fast Finish Run 6	Foundation Run 6 or Cross-Train	Foundation Run 5 or Cross-Train	Hill Repetition Run 6	Recovery Run 6 or Cross-Train	Long Run 5	L: 88% M/H: 12%

(continued)

	MON	TUE	WED	THU	FRI	SAT	SUN	INTENSITY BALANCE
				PEAK PHASE				
10	Foundation Run 6 or Cross-Train	Cruise Interval Run 1	Recovery Run 6 or Cross-Train	Foundation Run 6 or Cross-Train	Short Interval Run 4	Recovery Run 6 or Cross-Train	Long Run 13	L: 84% M/H: 16%
11	Recovery Run 6 or Cross-Train	Tempo Run 4	Recovery Run 6 or Cross-Train	Foundation Run 6 or Cross-Train	Short Interval Run 5	Recovery Run 6 or Cross-Train	Long Run 15	L: 86% M/H: 14%
12		Tempo Run 3	Recovery Run 5	Foundation Run 5	Short Interval Run 3	Recovery Run 5	Long Run 7	L: 85% M/H: 15%
13	Foundation Run 6 or Cross-Train	Tempo Run 5	Recovery Run 6 or Cross-Train	Foundation Run 6 or Cross-Train	Long Interval Run 3	Recovery Run 6 or Cross-Train	Long Run with Speed Play 4	L: 80% M/H: 20%
14	Recovery Run 6 or Cross-Train	Cruise Interval Run 2	Recovery Run 6 or Cross-Train	Foundation Run 6 or Cross-Train	Long Interval Run 5	Recovery Run 6 or Cross-Train	Long Run with Fast Finish 4	L: 79% M/H: 21%
15		Tempo Run 4	Recovery Run 5 or Cross-Train	Foundation Run 5 or Cross-Train	Long Interval Run 2	Recovery Run 5 or Cross-Train	Marathon Simulator Run	L: 77% M/H: 23%
16	Recovery Run 6 or Cross-Train	Tempo Run 6	Recovery Run 6 or Cross-Train	Foundation Run 6 or Cross-Train	Mixed Interval Run 2	Recovery Run 6 or Cross-Train	Long Run with Speed Play 5	L: 78% M/H: 22%
				TAPER PHASE				
17	Recovery Run 5 or Cross-Train	Cruise Intervals 1	Foundation Run 4 or Cross-Train	Foundation Run 4 or Cross-Train	Mixed Interval Run 1	Recovery Run 4 or Cross-Train	Long Run with Fast Finish	L: 82% M/H: 18%

	MON	TUE	WED	THU	FRI	SAT	SUN	INTENSITY BALANCE
18		Fast Finish Run 4	Foundation Run 3 or Cross-Train	Foundation Run 3 or Cross-Train	Speed Play Run 3	Recovery Run 1	Marathon	L: 83% M/H: 17%

LEVEL 3

This plan is a good fit for experienced competitive runners who are prepared to train twice a day some days in pursuit of improved marathon performance. Before you begin the plan, build your training to the point where you are running at least three times per week, including some short efforts at moderate and high intensities and some easy runs of at least ten miles and where you are doing aerobic exercise at least seven times per week. The training load starts at 6 hours and 43 minutes in Week 1 and peaks at about 10 hours and 51 minutes in Week 16.

	MON	TUE	WED	THU	FRI	SAT	SUN	INTENSITY BALANCE
				BASE PHASE				
1	Foundation Run 6 or Cross-Train	Fast Finish Run 6 / Foundation Run 3 or Cross-Train	Foundation Run 6 or Cross-Train	Foundation Run 6 or Cross-Train	Speed Play Run 6	Foundation Run 6 or Cross-Train	Long Run 5	L: 92% M/H: 8

(continued)

	MON	TUE	WED	THU	FRI	SAT	SUN	INTENSITY BALANCE
2	Foundation Run 6 or Cross-Train	Fast Finish Run 6 Foundation Run 3 or Cross-Train	Foundation Run 6 or Cross-Train	Foundation Run 6 or Cross-Train Foundation Run 3 or Cross-Train	Speed Play Run 10	Foundation Run 6 or Cross-Train	Long Run 7	L: 91% M/H: 9%
3		Fast Finish Run 6 Foundation Run 3 or Cross-Train	Foundation Run 6 or Cross-Train	Foundation Run 6 or Cross-Train	Speed Play Run 8	Foundation Run 6 or Cross-Train	Long Run 5	L: 87% M/H: 13%
4	Foundation Run 6 or Cross-Train	Fast Finish Run 7 Foundation Run 4 or Cross-Train	Foundation Run 6 or Cross-Train	Foundation Run 6 or Cross-Train Foundation Run 4 or Cross-Train	Hill Repetition Run 7	Recovery Run 6 or Cross-Train	Long Run 9	L: 94% M/H: 6%
5	Foundation Run 6 or Cross-Train	Fast Finish Run 8 Foundation Run 4 or Cross-Train	Foundation Run 7 or Cross-Train	Foundation Run 6 or Cross-Train Foundation Run 4 or Cross-Train	Hill Repetition Run 8	Recovery Run 6 or Cross-Train Foundation Run 4 or Cross-Train	Long Run 11	L: 90% M/H: 10%

	MON	TUE	WED	THU	FRI	SAT	SUN	INTENSITY BALANCE
6		Fast Finish Run 7	Foundation Run 6 or Cross-Train	Foundation Run 6 or Cross-Train	Hill Repetition Run 6	Recovery Run 6 or Cross-Train	Long Run 7	L: 90% M/H: 10%
		Foundation Run 4 or Cross-Train		Foundation Run 4 or Cross-Train				
7	Foundation Run 6 or Cross-Train	Fast Finish Run 9	Foundation Run 7 or Cross-Train	Foundation Run 6 or Cross-Train	Hill Repetition Run 9	Recovery Run 6 or Cross-Train	Long Run 13	L: 89% M/H: 11%
		Foundation Run 5 or Cross-Train		Foundation Run 5 or Cross-Train		Foundation Run 5 or Cross-Train		
8	Foundation Run 6 or Cross-Train	Fast Finish Run 10	Foundation Run 7 or Cross-Train	Foundation Run 6 or Cross-Train	Hill Repetition Run 11	Recovery Run 6 or Cross-Train	Long Run 15	L: 90% M/H: 10%
		Foundation Run 6 or Cross-Train		Foundation Run 6 or Cross-Train		Foundation Run 6 or Cross-Train		

(continued)

	MON	TUE	WED	THU	FRI	SAT	SUN	INTENSITY BALANCE
9		Fast Finish Run 9	Foundation Run 6 or Cross-Train	Foundation Run 5 or Cross-Train	Hill Repetition Run 6	Recovery Run 5 or Cross-Train	Long Run 8	L: 92% M/H: 8%
		Foundation Run 5 or Cross-Train		Foundation Run 5 or Cross-Train		Foundation Run 5 or Cross-Train		
PEAK PHASE								
10	Foundation Run 6 or Cross-Train	Cruise Interval Run 2	Foundation Run 8 or Cross-Train	Foundation Run 6 or Cross-Train	Short Interval Run 7	Recovery Run 6 or Cross-Train	Long Run with Speed Play 4	L: 80% M/H: 20%
		Recovery Run 6 or Cross-Train		Foundation Run 6 or Cross-Train		Foundation Run 6 or Cross-Train		
11	Recovery Run 6 or Cross-Train	Tempo Run 8	Foundation Run 8 or Cross-Train	Foundation Run 6 or Cross-Train	Short Interval Run 8	Recovery Run 6 or Cross-Train	Long Run with Fast Finish 4	L: 83% M/H: 17%
		Recovery Run 6 or Cross-Train		Foundation Run 6 or Cross-Train		Foundation Run 6 or Cross-Train		

	MON	TUE	WED	THU	FRI	SAT	SUN	INTENSITY BALANCE
12		Cruise Interval Run 2	Foundation Run 6 or Cross-Train	Foundation Run 5 or Cross-Train	Short Interval Run 4	Recovery Run 5 or Cross-Train	Long Run with Speed Play 3	L: 80% M/H: 20%
		Recovery Run 5 or Cross-Train		Foundation Run 5 or Cross-Train		Foundation Run 5 or Cross-Train		
13	Recovery Run 6 or Cross-Train	Cruise Interval Run 3	Foundation Run 9 or Cross-Train	Foundation Run 6 or Cross-Train	Long Interval Run 6	Recovery Run 6 or Cross-Train	Long Run with Speed Play 5	L: 81% M/H: 19%
		Recovery Run 6 or Cross-Train		Foundation Run 6 or Cross-Train		Foundation Run or Cross-Train		
14	Recovery Run 6 or Cross-Train	Tempo Run 9	Foundation Run 9 or Cross-Train	Foundation Run 6 or Cross-Train	Long Interval Run 7	Recovery Run 6 or Cross-Train	Long Run with Speed Play 6	L: 81% M/H: 19%
		Recovery Run 6 or Cross-Train		Foundation Run 6 or Cross-Train		Foundation Run 6 or Cross-Train		

(continued)

	MON	TUE	WED	THU	FRI	SAT	SUN	INTENSITY BALANCE
15		Tempo Run 4	Foundation Run 6 or Cross-Train	Foundation Run 5 or Cross-Train	Long Interval Run 4	Recovery Run 5 or Cross-Train	Marathon Simulator Run	L: 80% M/H: 20%
		Recovery Run 5 or Cross-Train		Foundation Run 5 or Cross-Train		Foundation Run 5 or Cross-Train		
16	Recovery Run 6 or Cross-Train	Cruise Interval Run 4	Foundation Run 9 or Cross-Train	Foundation Run 6 or Cross-Train	Mixed Interval Run 4	Recovery Run 6 or Cross-Train	Long Run with Fast Finish 6	L: 80% M/H: 20%
		Recovery Run 6 or Cross-Train		Foundation Run 6 or Cross-Train		Foundation Run 6 or Cross-Train		
TAPER PHASE								
17	Recovery Run 5 or Cross-Train	Tempo Run 6	Foundation Run 5 or Cross-Train	Foundation Run 5 or Cross-Train	Mixed Interval Run 2	Recovery Run 4 or Cross-Train	Long Run with Speed Play 3	L: 82% M/H: 18%
		Recovery Run 5 or Cross-Train		Foundation Run 4 or Cross-Train		Foundation Run 4 or Cross-Train		
18		Fast Finish Run 6	Foundation Run 5 or Cross-Train	Foundation Run 4 or Cross-Train	Speed Play Run 5	Recovery Run 2	Marathon	L: 80% M/H: 20%

CROSS-TRAINING AS AN ALTERNATIVE TO RUNNING MORE

The primary benefit of training by the 80/20 Rule is better fitness. You will get fitter from the same amount of running if you keep the intensity low roughly 80 percent of the time. A secondary benefit of obeying the 80/20 Rule is that it enables runners to train more. If you take advantage of this opportunity, you will experience additional improvement.

Training more doesn't necessarily mean running more. The problem with running more is that increased running volume brings with it increased injury risk. The high-impact nature of running makes it rather hard on the body compared to other, nonimpact aerobic activities. Cyclists and swimmers suffer overuse injuries too, but not nearly as often as runners do. Consider this: A 1998 study conducted by researchers at England's Straffordshire University found that among triathletes—who, of course, do a mix of swimming, cycling, and running—more than 60 percent of all injuries suffered over a five-year period were running related. Swimming and cycling together accounted for the other 40 percent.

Some runners are very durable and can run as much as they like without getting injured. If you're one of these runners, you can go ahead and train more by running more. If you're like many other runners, however, who tend to break down when they take chances on mileage, take heart: You can work around this limitation by supplementing your running with cycling or another form of nonimpact aerobic exercise. Studies have shown that runners who cross-train more are indeed less likely to get injured. Research also suggests that adding cross-training to a running program boosts performance almost as much as additional running does. In 1998, Mick Flynn and colleagues at Purdue University added either three extra runs or three stationary bike workouts to the training programs of twenty runners for a period of six weeks. All of the runners completed a 5K time trial before this period of modified training and again afterward. Both the running-only group and the cross-training group improved their times by an average of 2.5 percent.

Although fitness gained through cycling and similar activities clearly transfers well to running, cross-training is not a perfect substitute for running. (If it were, you could maximize your running performance without running at all.) One benefit of running that cycling and other alternatives can't match is improvement in *running skill*. As we saw in chapter 6, triathletes who train as much as runners do are just as fit but exhibit less relaxed smooth ease because they don't get as much practice with the running stride. Nevertheless, the effects of cross-training on running performance are significant enough that even some professional runners do it in large amounts. For example, Adriana Nelson Pirtea, a Romanian-born American runner, spends a lot of time on an outdoor elliptical bike (i.e., an elliptical trainer on wheels, or a seatless bicycle), which helped her win the 2013 USA Half Marathon Championships with a superb time of 1:11:19.

World-class runners like Pirtea have more time and more incentive to train than other runners do. If you're like most recreational runners, there's only so much time you're willing to put into chasing PRs. But chances are it's not really a lack of willingness that is holding you back from training at least a bit more than you do now. It's more likely that you just don't feel able to do more. Either you lack the energy or you fear getting injured or both.

Following the 80/20 Rule will solve the energy problem. Runners who switch from the typical 50/50 intensity ratio to an 80/20 balance invariably discover that they can easily handle a few extra miles of running. Incorporating cross-training into your regimen will solve the problem of injury risk. Only you can decide how much time you are comfortable devoting to exercise. As a coach, I want you to be the best runner you can be, so I encourage you to train *no less than* the maximum amount you are willing to do. In other words, I don't want you to be limited by any factor other than your personal priorities. In this chapter, I will show you how to eliminate the injury barrier by adding cross-training to your 80/20 running program.

TWO APPROACHES TO CROSS-TRAINING

I believe that most runners, including those who seldom get injured, should do at least one nonimpact cardio workout per week when healthy. The reason is that runners who make cross-training a part of their normal routine are more prepared physically and psychologically to fall back on an alternative form of exercise in times of crisis.

On the psychological side, runners who cross-train only when they are injured have a greater tendency to run when they shouldn't. Lacking a ready fallback option, they try to push through pain instead of taking the cautious route and hitting the elliptical trainer (or whatever) instead. Runners who don't wait until they are hurt to cross-train tend to be more comfortable with the idea of replacing *all* of their runs with nonimpact aerobic workouts when it's the wise thing to do.

Often, runners who cross-train only when injured are also ill prepared physically to transfer their training regimen from running to an alternative activity when necessary. It takes time for the musculoskeletal system to adapt to any form of exercise. If you immediately go from running every day to, say, cycling every day because of any injury, there's a good chance you will also suffer a cycling-related overuse injury. If you've been riding a bike once a week all along, though, your body will be able to make the adjustment smoothly.

If your only purpose in cross-training is to get your mind and body prepared to rely exclusively on cross-training to maintain fitness when you're injured, then it is enough to merely *replace* one of your weekly runs with a nonimpact alternative. But my goal here is to encourage you to use cross-training for the additional purpose of increasing your overall training volume and enhancing your fitness. To fulfill this purpose, you must incorporate cross-training into your program in a manner that increases your overall training volume.

There are two general approaches to doing this: "minimalist" and "aggressive." One of the two will be right for you.

The Minimalist Approach

The minimalist method entails adding a single cross-training session to your current running schedule. Suppose, for example, you are currently running five times per week. If you add one cross-training workout to your regimen, you will increase your training volume by 20 percent without subjecting your legs to any additional impact stress. Trust me: You will get a noticeable boost from this investment, yet your injury risk will change only marginally.

This is a good option for runners who don't want to add a lot of additional training time to their schedule or who wish to "dip their toes" into cross-training before taking the full plunge. But it's also a good fit for durable, high-mileage runners who are already doing about as much running as their body can handle and wish to use cross-training to raise their fitness level one more notch without subjecting their legs to any additional pounding. Many elite runners do just one cross-training workout per week to supplement one hundred miles or more of running.

The Aggressive Approach

The aggressive approach to cross-training is also the cautious approach. It is aggressive in the sense that it entails including multiple cross-training workouts in the weekly training routine for the sake of increasing fitness. Yet at the same time, it is cautious in the sense that most runners who take this approach simultaneously reduce the amount of running they do to minimize injury risk and/or general wear and tear on the legs.

The typical aggressive cross-trainer is a highly competitive runner who has been frustrated by repeated injuries. Most runners don't trust the benefits of cross-training enough to give it a large and permanent place in their training routine until a series of breakdowns leaves them desperate and ready to try anything to break the cycle. Those who take a chance on the aggressive approach are often pleasantly surprised. Indeed, there are some noteworthy examples of top runners who have drastically reduced their running volume without any loss of performance because cross-training has successfully filled the gap.

The poster boy of the aggressive approach to cross-training is Meb Keflezighi, who in 2009 became the first American to win the New York City Marathon since Alberto Salazar in 1982. Less durable than many of his rivals, Meb used various nonimpact forms of cross-training throughout his career both to stay fit when he was hurt and to supplement a reduced-mileage running regimen when he was healthy. In 2013, when he was thirty-seven years old, Keflezighi was forced to withdraw from the Boston Marathon with a calf injury. While it healed, he spent a lot of time riding an outdoor elliptical bike and a regular bike. When the healing was complete, Meb shifted to a schedule of running once a day in the morning and doing a nonimpact aerobic workout in the afternoon. Meb was still healthy and as fit as he'd ever been when the Boston Marathon came around again in April, two weeks shy of his thirty-ninth birthday. He won the race in a career-best time of 2:08:37, defeating a strong elite field that included the world's two top-ranked marathoners from the previous year.

The aggressive approach to cross-training is suitable not only for injury-prone runners of all ages but also for any runner over the age of thirty-five who wishes to protect his or her legs from some of the cumulative effects of many years of high-mileage running. It is an unfortunate reality that runners slow down with age at a steeper rate than other endurance athletes do. Scientists don't know exactly why this is the case, but experienced older runners often report feeling as though years of high-mileage training has taken some of the "bounce" out of their legs. This is a scientifically plausible explanation because running performance depends on a certain kind of bounciness whereas performance in other, nonimpact endurance disciplines does not.

In cycling and swimming, the best athletes over the age of forty are typically the same men and women who were the best in their sport when they were in their early twenties. Running is different. Most of the masters world records in running are held by runners who started late. Kathryn Martin, for example, took up running at age thirty and subsequently rewrote the U.S. record book in the 50-to-54 and 55-to-59 age groups. Martin's male counterpart, Ed Whitlock, did some running as a schoolboy but only got serious in middle age. When he was seventy-three years old, Whitlock ran a marathon in 2:54:48.

Runners who were the best in the world in their twenties and who keep competing past middle age are almost never the top competitors in the older age groups. Most are still very good, of course, but they slow down precipitously after age forty-five and are eclipsed by late starters like Martin and Whitlock. Bill Rodgers was one of the fastest marathon runners in the world in his prime, but between his fiftieth and sixtieth birthdays, his 10K time slowed by a staggering ten minutes. By the end of that slide, Rodgers was no longer among the fastest runners his age in America.

There is limited evidence that prolonged high-mileage running accelerates muscle aging in a way that might explain why many older runners feel that years of pounding the pavement have made their stride less bouncy. In 2010, Dale Rae and colleagues at the University of Cape Town measured the length of DNA strands extracted from the calf muscles of a group of experienced middle-aged runners. Scientists measure the length of DNA strands inside of cells to assess physiological age. Time and stress cause our DNA to progressively shorten. Rae's team discovered a significant inverse correlation between running experience and habitual training volume, on the one hand, and DNA length, on the other. In other words, within this group of experienced middle-aged runners, those who had the fewest miles in their legs had the "youngest" DNA.

It's important not to overinterpret this finding, however. When Rae and his colleagues compared the average length of muscle cell DNA in middle-aged runners to that of age-matched nonrunners, they found no difference. So there's no need for runners in their twenties to panic and run less than they would otherwise. But I do think it's sensible for experienced runners to transition to doing more cross-training and less running after age thirty-five. Those who do so stand to extend their peak performance years and ultimately reduce the rate at which their performance declines.

There are many ways to balance running and cross-training within the aggressive approach. The more concerned you are with maximizing performance, the more cross-training workouts you should do. The more concerned you are with reducing injury risk or wear and tear on your legs, the fewer runs you should do. Three runs per week should be considered a minimum; it's hard to make any progress as a runner if you run less than every other day or so, no matter how much you cross-train. A sensible upper limit for total workouts in a week (running plus cross-training) is thirteen—that's two workouts per day on six days of the week plus one workout on a designated recovery day. Of these thirteen workouts, no more than six or seven need to be runs, even if you're 100 percent committed to becoming the best runner you can be. If Meb Keflezighi can run a 2:08 marathon on seven runs per week (plus an equal number of cross-training sessions), then surely you can achieve your goals with a similar regimen.

I recommend that you increase the total number of workouts in your typical training week by no more than one or two sessions at a time. Abrupt increases in overall training volume are likely to cause burnout even if the additional workouts are nonimpact and don't increase injury risk. Let's say you're currently running six times per week. From here you might switch to a schedule of six runs and one cross-training workout or five runs and two cross-training workouts. If your body tolerates the increased training load well, you may then move to a schedule of eight or nine total workouts per week.

Table 12.1 presents a full range of different ways to balance running and cross-training with either the aggressive approach or the minimalist and provides information about the type of runner that is the best match for each specific option. You may need to experiment a bit to find the balance that's best for you. Be aware too that the ideal balance may change over time. When in doubt about what to do, err on the side of more cross-training (because more volume equals more fitness) and less running (because less running means less injury risk).

Regardless of how you choose to balance running and cross-training, it's essential that you apply the 80/20 Rule to your total training regimen, not just your running. If you run four hours per week and cycle two hours per week, for example, the total amount of moderate- and high-intensity training you do each week should be about seventy-two minutes, or 20 percent of six hours. It is not necessary, however, to follow the 80/20 Rule in running and cross-training individually. On the contrary, I believe it's best to do your hardest work in the discipline you're actually preparing to compete in. Therefore I advise you to do all of your cross-training workouts at low intensity and concentrate your full allotment of moderate- and high-intensity training within your runs. So again, if you run four hours per week and

TABLE 12.1   SOME WAYS TO BALANCE RUNNING AND CROSS-TRAINING

RUNS PER WEEK	CROSS-TRAINING SESSIONS PER WEEK	SUITABLE FOR YOU IF . . .
"MINIMALIST" OPTIONS		
5–6	1	You're a beginner or You're not superfit or You need or prefer a less time-intensive training schedule and You're not especially injury prone
7–12	1	You're an experienced, competitive runner *and* You're not especially injury prone
"AGGRESSIVE" OPTIONS		
3–4	3–4	You're a beginner or You're not superfit or You need or prefer a less time-intensive training schedule and You are injury prone or over thirty-five years old
3–7	5–10	You're an experienced, competitive runner and You are injury prone or over thirty-five years old

cycle two hours, I suggest you do seventy-two minutes of running per week at moderate and high intensity and the full two hours you spend on the bike at low intensity.

Exempt yourself from this advice, however, if you are prone to suffering injuries such as Achilles tendon strains and hamstring strains that are associated with faster running. In this case, concentrate your full allotment of moderate- and high-intensity training within your chosen cross-training discipline.

If you're already injured and currently unable to run, your best course of action is to replace each planned run on your schedule with a cross-training version of the same workout. So, for example, if you were supposed to do a dozen 60-second hill repetitions in Zone 5 on a given day but you can't because your knee hurts, do a similar session on your bike instead.

You can use the same tools to monitor and control intensity in cross-training workouts as you do in your runs. Note, however, that heart rate zones differ slightly from one activity to the next. The lactate threshold heart rate is generally about ten beats per minute higher in running than it is in most nonimpact alternatives. So if you use a heart rate monitor to regulate intensity in cross-training workouts, you'll first need to do a thirty-minute time trial, perceived effort test, or talk test in that activity and use the results to calculate zones that are specific to it.

THE SEVEN BEST CROSS-TRAINING ACTIVITIES FOR RUNNERS

There are many forms of nonimpact aerobic exercise. Some are better than others for runners. As you might expect, those that are most similar to running have the greatest fitness carryover to running. Activities that involve alternating movements of the legs, such as cycling, work very well. Upper-body dominant activities such swimming do not.

Support for the specificity principle in cross-training comes from a clever study conducted by French researchers in 2002. A group of elite triathletes was monitored for forty weeks. Training volume was tracked separately in each discipline. Every few weeks, the subjects completed performance tests in the pool, on the bike, and on the treadmill. When all of the data had been collected, the researchers compared the volume of training in each discipline against performance in all three disciplines. These cross-correlations allowed the researchers to estimate the effect of, say, swim training not just on swimming performance but also on cycling and running performance. Not surprisingly, the researchers found that bike training had a strong positive effect on running performance, but swimming did not.

Cycling is not the only effective form of cross-training for runners, however. There are seven forms of nonimpact aerobic exercise (including cycling) that stand out of from the rest. Each has advantages and disadvantages relative to the others, but you can't go wrong with any of them. Consider factors such as your personal likes and dislikes, convenience, and budget when deciding which activity is right for you. If, for example, you live in an urban area where cycling is a hassle but you happen to own a treadmill, then uphill treadmill walking might be your best option. In Table 8.2, I grade each cross-training activity on the three key factors of running specificity, convenience, and enjoyableness.

It's okay to do more than one form of cross-training. I myself ride an elliptical bike and a regular bike, and I do some uphill treadmill walking as well, because I enjoy all three activities and I enjoy cross-training more in general when my routine is varied.

Antigravity Treadmill Running

Technically, antigravity treadmill running is not an alternative to running—it's an alternative form of running. The machine that it's done on consists of a normal treadmill with a tentlike enclosure attached to it. The user steps through a hole at the top of the enclosure and zips himself or herself in around the waist, creating an airtight seal. The chamber is then pressurized, and this high-pressure zone gently lifts the runner, effectively reducing the force of gravity within it.

The amount of pressure is adjustable, enabling the user to run at anywhere between 20 percent and 100 percent of his or her actual body weight. The lower the user goes within this range, the less pounding the body is subjected to. The intensity of the workout also decreases with effective body weight, so it's necessary to run faster than normal to get an equivalent workout on an antigravity treadmill.

Runners who use these machines for supplemental training usually run at an effective body weight of 90 to 95 percent. But most are professionals who are very light to begin with. Settings in the range of 80 to 85 percent of full body weight are preferable for heavier or less durable recreational runners. You might as well err on the low side because you can always adjust your speed to get your heart rate up to where it would normally be for the type of workout you're doing. One study found that by running faster on an antigravity treadmill, runners were able to get their maximum rate of oxygen consumption just as high at 85 percent of their body weight as they were at their full body weight.

The chief advantage of antigravity treadmill running is that it is more like normal running than any other form of cross-training. Therefore it probably enhances running performance more effectively than the other options do. (I say "probably" because this conjecture has not been formally tested.)

Antigravity treadmills also have an advantage for injured runners. Because running on an antigravity treadmill is a low-impact activity instead of a nonimpact activity, it does a better job of helping injured runners maintain their adaptations to repetitive impact (such as increased bone density) during prolonged periods of rehabilitation. This leaves them less likely to develop a new injury when they return to normal running.

It is possible to "train through" almost any injury on an antigravity treadmill. All you have to do is keep reducing the effective body weight setting until you're able to run pain-free. As you heal, you can gradually increase your effective body weight, always using pain as your guide, until you are able to run normally again.

The major disadvantages of antigravity treadmills are cost and accessibility. Currently there is only one manufacturer, the technology's inventor, Alter-G. The cheaper of the two models that the company offers goes for $25,000, which is more than most runners are willing or able to spend. Some physical therapy clinics and fitness facilities rent out time on antigravity treadmills, but even if there is such a facility relatively close to your home, this is not the most convenient or affordable way to cross-train.

Another disadvantage of antigravity treadmill running is that it's rather boring. I once spent several hours over a two-day period running on an Alter-G that was set up at a trade show booth belonging to a company I was affiliated with. Those hours felt like days.

Bicycling

Cycling is not nearly as running specific as antigravity treadmill running. Whereas cycling is a seated activity, running is upright. On the bike, the quadriceps act as prime movers, but in running they are used primarily as shock absorbers. Despite such differences, there is abundant scientific and real-world evidence that cycling fitness transfers well to running.

There are two ways to ride a bike: outdoors on roads or trails and indoors on a stationary machine. Outdoor riding is generally regarded as being more enjoyable while indoor riding is more convenient, especially in foul weather. It's also less intimidating for the technically inept runner (like me) who takes twenty minutes to fix a flat tire.

If you intend to do a lot of cycling, it's important that you use a bike that fits you properly. A proper bike fit is much more complex than a proper running shoe fit. Getting the right size is only the beginning. On top of this you need to make sure your saddle height, saddle fore-aft position, crank arm length, handlebar position, and several other settings are dialed in just right. This requires that you get a professional fitting from a certified bike fitter. Putting in a lot of miles with the seat just a centimeter too high or too low or with some other setting just slightly off is likely to result in knee pain, lower-back pain, or other common cycling overuse injuries.

Outdoor Elliptical Biking

An elliptical bike is like the elliptical trainers you see at every gym except that it has two wheels and is ridden outdoors. The machine was invented by a Southern California outfit called ElliptiGO. The company's founders happen to be friends of mine, and I was an early adopter of the technology. Call me biased, but if I had to name one cross-training activity for runners as the best overall, outdoor elliptical biking would be my choice.

The standard indoor elliptical trainer was invented specifically to simulate the running action without impact, so there's no question that fitness earned on the outdoor version transfers well to running. The big advantage of outdoor elliptical biking is that it's really fun. After twenty minutes on an indoor elliptical trainer, I'm about ready to scream, but I routinely take my ElliptiGO for two- and three-hour rides and enjoy every minute. Fun matters. The more you enjoy a cross-training activity, the more time you'll be willing to put into it, and the more fitness you'll get out of it.

Within the past several years, outdoor elliptical biking has become quite trendy among professional runners in the United States. In addition to Adriana Nelson Pirtea and Meb Keflezighi, whom I've mentioned already, 2012 Olympian Julie Culley, two-time USA outdoor 5000-meter champion Lauren Fleshman, 2000 Olympian Adam Goucher, 5000-meter American record holder Molly Huddle, five-time USA outdoor 800-meter champion Alysia Montaño, and 2:29 marathoner Stephanie Rothstein have all been spotted zooming around on ElliptiGO bikes.

Outdoor elliptical training has two potential drawbacks. One is cost. ElliptiGO bikes are made with racing-quality materials and parts, so they aren't cheap: $2,200 and up. There are cheaper elliptical bikes on the market, but they are not suitable for serious cross-training. The other potential downside of outdoor elliptical biking is that it is not a practicable option in all environments and weather conditions. If you live in an area with very narrow road shoulders or long, icy winters, outdoor elliptical biking is not the best cross-training option for you.

Indoor Elliptical Training

The standard indoor elliptical trainer has become something of a redheaded stepchild since the advent of the outdoor elliptical bike, but it's still a great form of running-specific cross-training. Convenience is a major plus of the activity: As an indoor pursuit, elliptical training can be done anytime, and if you have a gym membership, you have ready access to high-quality elliptical trainers. The only drawback of indoor elliptical training is the boredom factor.

Pool Running

Pool running, which entails simulating a normal running action while running in deep water, used to be the go-to cross-training activity for injured elite runners. It has since lost popularity to newer alternatives such as antigravity treadmill running and outdoor elliptical biking, but some elite runners still use pool running for cool-downs after long runs to pad their training volume without increasing injury risk.

The main advantage of pool running is that when done correctly, it very closely simulates the action of overground running. For this reason fitness developed through pool running transfers well to normal running. One study found that runners were able to fully maintain their fitness level with six weeks of exclusive pool running.

When running in water, you should make your best effort to mimic a natural overground running stride as closely as possible. This is next to impossible if you're not wearing a pool running vest such as those made by AquaJogger, which do the work of keeping you afloat so you can concentrate on using your arms and legs to simulate normal running. These products cost $40 to $60 and are available at many running specialty stores.

The big difference between overground running and pool running is that the former is a closed-chain activity, meaning there is contact with the ground, whereas pool running is an open-chain activity with no weight bearing whatsoever. If you do nothing but pool running for exercise during a period of injury, therefore, you will lose bone density in your legs as well as other adaptations to repetitive impact, and as a result, you will be at greater risk of suffering a new injury when you return to normal running. So it's best to mix pool running with a weight-bearing activity such as elliptical training during extended periods of injury rehabilitation. If you have an injury such as a stress fracture that prevents you from doing any form of weight-bearing activity, however, then pool running could be a lifesaver.

As a supplement to running itself, pool running rates lower than other options on the fun scale. Indeed, I rate it as the dullest form of cross-training I've ever tried (and I've tried them all), nor have I ever met a runner who says he or she loves the activity.

Slideboarding

Few runners have ever heard of slideboarding. A slideboard is a long rectangular plastic surface upon which the user slides from side to side between bumpers positioned at either end while wearing special fabric booties, thus simulating a skating motion. Slideboarding is typically done by hockey players and speed skaters when they can't get on the ice to train.

Slideboarding offers a number of advantages as a cross-training activity for runners. It provides an excellent aerobic-training stimulus through a weight-bearing action involving alternating use of the legs, just like running. It is also convenient. A slideboard contains no moving or metal parts, it can be laid out anywhere in your home and rolled up for storage when you're done, and you can even travel with one. Slideboards are also far less expensive than other home exercise products. I got mine for $249. What's more, I find slideboarding much more fun than other indoor aerobic activities—almost as enjoyable as actual ice-skating.

The big difference between slideboarding and running is that running is a forward movement whereas slideboarding is a lateral movement. But even this difference counts as a positive. Slideboarding strengthens the muscles on the inside and outside of the hips that tend to be weak in runners and whose weakness often contributes to knee injuries. Despite its lack of familiarity, slideboarding is a great cross-training choice for runners who prize convenience and affordability and are susceptible to knee pain.

Uphill Treadmill Walking

Walking was the original form of cross-training for runners. Until the 1940s, most competitive distance runners did some walking as part of their training. The practice died out, though, after Arthur Lydiard decided that slow running was more beneficial than walking. When cross-training made a comeback in the 1990s, walking was overlooked in favor of other activities such as elliptical training that seemed to better match the intensity of running. But there is a particular form of walking that does not suffer from this drawback: uphill treadmill walking.

Uphill treadmill walking is better than regular walking in two ways. First, while it's hard to get the heart rate up into the Zone 2 range on an outdoor walk in most environments, with uphill treadmill walking it's easy. Second, uphill treadmill walking is more similar to running on a neuromuscular level. Research has shown that when a person is moving up a steep incline at the precise speed at which he or she feels the urge to transition from a walking gate to a running stride, the brain uses the same motor pattern to produce either movement. In other words, the distinction between walking and running effectively disappears.

If you're skeptical, try this experiment: Hop on a treadmill, set the belt at a 15 percent incline, and start walking slowly. Next, increase your speed in small increments until you feel an urge to transition to running. At this point, go ahead and start running. After a few moments, go back to walking. You will notice that your movements are not actually changing. Even when you tell yourself you're running, you always have one foot in contact with the ground, as in walking.

For most runners, the speed at which this walk-run convergence occurs falls within the moderate-intensity or even the high-intensity range, so it's too fast for cross-training workouts. But even slow walking on a steep incline is more running specific than most other forms of cross-training. I do it at least a couple of times every week, and the fitness transfer to running is palpable.

When you first try uphill treadmill walking, you will have to play around with different speeds and gradients to find those that place you in Zones 1 and 2. Be sure to keep your first few sessions relatively short to avoid straining your calf muscles and Achilles tendons. After a couple of weeks, these tissues will be fully adapted to the activity.

Uphill treadmill walking has the potential to be boring, but it's seldom boring for me because I read while I'm doing it. I get through a book a week this way. There's nothing like giving your brain and your body a workout at the same time!

TABLE 8.2   **RELATIVE MERITS OF THE SEVEN BEST CROSS-TRAINING ACTIVITIES FOR RUNNERS**

	RUNNING SPECIFICITY	CONVENIENCE	ENJOYABLENESS
Antigravity Treadmill Running	A	D	C–
Bicycling	B–	B	B+
Outdoor Elliptical Biking	B+	B	A
Indoor Elliptical Training	B	B+	D+
Pool Running	B–	B–	D
Slideboarding	C+	A	B–
Uphill Treadmill Walking	B+	B+	C+

YOUR CROSS-TRAINING ROUTINE

When you design your next training plan, consider slightly increasing the average amount of training you do compared to your past routine. Decide how many total workouts per week you'll need to do to effect this increase and how many of these workouts will be cross-training sessions. Also settle on one or more specific nonrunning activities you will rely on for supplemental aerobic training. Plan to maintain a consistent schedule of cross-training and running workouts from week to week throughout the training process so that your body can get used to it.

The training plans presented in chapters 8 through 11 were designed to facilitate this approach. First of all, they prescribe higher volume than most training plans intended for mass consumption. They also have built-in flexibility in terms of how much of the prescribed training takes the form of running. Choose the days on which you will exercise the option to cross-train before you begin to execute any of these plans.

Remember, however, to treat your plan as just that: a plan. If you're ever too sore to run on a given day when you have a run planned, make a spontaneous switch to cross-training. Likewise, if you develop a running-related injury, replace all of your planned runs with low-impact or nonimpact alternatives. Because you will have been cross-training all along, this adjustment, should it be required, won't be difficult for you, either physically or psychologically.

13.

80/20 FOR EVERYONE?

Lots of people take up running as a way to lose weight. In a recent survey by Running USA, "concerns about weight" ranked as the second most commonly cited reason for starting a running program, behind only the generic "for exercise." Research indicates that running is a smart choice for the weight-loss seeker. Numerous studies have shown that people who select running as their primary form of exercise lose more weight than do people who choose other fitness activities.

In a 2012 study, for example, Paul Williams of the Lawrence Berkeley National Laboratory compared the effects of running and other forms of exercise on body mass index (BMI) and waist circumference in a population of more than thirty-three thousand men and women. He found that the waist-reducing effect of running in women was 9.5 times greater than that of other forms of exercise, and in men the BMI-reducing effect of running was 19.3 times greater.

Why is running so much more effective for weight loss than other activities? Some experts believe it is because runners tend to measure their workouts in terms of distance covered instead of time elapsed. It takes the same amount of energy for a person of a given weight to run a mile at any speed, whereas the effectiveness of thirty minutes of Zumba or water aerobics depends on how much the exerciser puts into it. We've all seen people who go to the gym and float in the pool or move in apparent slow motion on a stair climbing machine, failing to get their heart rate up even into the low-intensity exercise range.

Yet running also yields more weight loss than activities such as walking and swimming that are typically measured by distance covered as well. So there must be some other factor at work. This other effect may have to do with running's effect on appetite. People tend to eat more after walking or swimming than they do after running.

This is all very interesting. But from the perspective of the average person looking to lose weight, it doesn't really matter *why* running works better. It's enough to know *that* it works better.

The goal of losing weight is, of course, rather different from the goal of getting in shape for races, which has been the focus of this book. We have seen that adhering to the 80/20 Rule is the most effective way to attain peak running fitness for competitive events. But is it also the most effective way to lose weight? As we shall see in this chapter, the best evidence from science and the real world indicates that it is.

While many people start running to lose weight, they keep running for other reasons. This shift is partly explained by the fact that people who keep running usually attain their weight-loss goals. But it is also explained in part by the fact that people whose primary motivation for running is weight loss tend to quit early. Running is hardly unique in this way. Weight loss is not a strong motivator for long-term adherence to any exercise program. Few people exercise consistently year after year unless they *enjoy* working out. Those new runners who eventually become seasoned runners do so because they develop a passion for running. Running USA reports that more than three-fifths of experienced runners cite "having fun" as one of the main reasons they keep at it.

Even the most passionate runners sometimes get bored with the same old routine, however. When they do, they often branch out from running into new challenges such as triathlon. Should runners who dabble in other endurance sports apply the 80/20 Rule in them as well? Again, the best evidence from science and the real world indicates they should.

80/20 WEIGHT LOSS

If you wander down to your local health club and hire a personal trainer to help you lose weight, there's a pretty good chance he or she will put you on a program that consists of three strength workouts and three "cardio" workouts per week. And it's also very likely that each of those cardio workouts will be a high-intensity interval session. How do I know? Because this has been the standard exercise formula for weight loss since Bill Phillips popularized it with his book *Body for Life* in 1999.

The absence of longer, less intense cardio workouts in this formula is easy to explain. Bill Phillips was a body builder. Like most body builders, Phillips looked at cardiovascular exercise as a necessary evil to be gotten over with as quickly as possible. The average personal trainer has the same mind-set. A passion for long trail runs is not likely to lead someone to take a job in a machine-packed, artificially lighted health club. Having little or no experience with low-intensity cardio exercise, personal trainers never think to include it in the programs they supply to their weight-loss clients.

The mass media have done their part to entrench the standard exercise formula for weight loss by hyping up high-intensity interval training as a time-saver. Fitness magazines and Web sites profit most when they tell people what they want to hear, and people want to hear that they can obtain the body of a professional athlete by spending less time working out than they do brushing their teeth. This point was made in a 2013 review of previous research on the use of high-intensity exercise for weight loss, whose author, Pierpaolo De Feo of the Healthy Lifestyle Institute in Perugia, Italy, wrote, "In our demanding society, the most attractive messages in the popular press are those promising the best results in a short time. This might explain the emphasis given by the media to those scientific articles that report the efficacy on weight loss of exercise programs [of] shorter duration and higher intensity."

While it's true that most people today are busy, nobody is really too busy to exercise. Surveys have shown that people who exercise regularly have just as much going on in their lives as do those who avoid exercise. The real reason why many new and prospective exercisers are attracted to short workouts is that they can't stand working out and therefore they wish to invest as little time in it as possible. The problem is that people who don't enjoy exercise *especially* don't enjoy high-intensity exercise. Once they have been exposed to the tortures of high-intensity interval training, most weight-loss seekers would gladly spend more time exercising at a lower intensity. Indeed, research has revealed that the dropout rate in high-intensity weight-loss exercise programs is significantly higher than it is in low-intensity programs.

Even when the factors of enjoyment and adherence are removed from the equation, an exercise program that combines a lot of low-intensity exercise with a little moderate- and high-intensity exercise is more effective for weight loss than is the standard interval-based formula. The main reason is that low-intensity exercise is significantly less stressful, so a person can tolerate far greater amounts of it without feeling overtaxed.

When scientists compare the effects of exercise at different intensities on weight loss, they usually match them by time or energy. They ask questions such as "Which program yields more weight loss: X minutes (or kilojoules) per week of low-intensity exercise or the same amount of high-intensity exercise?" But factors such as time and energy are not the true determinants of how much a person invests in his or her exercise routine. It is really done by feel—or, more precisely, by perceived effort. Each workout imposes a psychological burden on a person, which scientists measure with a tool called a *session RPE*. This variable is calculated by multiplying the athlete's overall sense of effort in a workout (as rated on a 1 to 10 scale) by the duration of the session in minutes. There is a limit to the cumulative amount of session RPE that a given exerciser is willing to tolerate from week to week, and this limit is the true determinant of each person's commitment to exercise.

Widespread testing of this tool has shown that relatively short high-intensity workouts feel just as challenging to runners as do very long low-intensity workouts that burn far greater numbers of calories. This is important, because the sum of session RPEs that an individual runner can tolerate from week to week is the same, regardless of whether he or she trains mostly at low intensity or mostly at high intensity. Runners therefore are able to burn far more total calories each week without exceeding their stress tolerance if they keep the intensity low most of the time.

Table 13.1 shows two running programs—an 80/20 program and a high-intensity program—that are about equal in terms of perceived stress but are very different in terms of the total number of calories burned. The 80/20 program does require a greater time commitment, but a runner who tries both schedules will not find the 80/20 program to be any more psychologically burdensome, yet it burns more than twice as many total calories.

Considering all of this, you might ask: "Why should I not do *all* of my training at low intensity if my goal as a runner is to lose as much weight as possible?" It's a good question with a simple answer. The reason it's better to include some running at higher intensities in a weight-loss program is that your overall fitness will improve more this way. And as your fitness improves, you will run faster and burn more calories at all intensities, even low intensity.

The comparison made in Table 13.1 is hypothetical, but it is consistent with what happens in the real world. Millions of men and women have succeeded in losing weight through running, and the vast majority of them have *not* done so with high-intensity interval-based programs. Indeed, I've never met anyone who has lost a lot of weight by sprinting on a treadmill at a health club under a personal

TABLE 13.1 **A COMPARISON OF TWO RUNNING PROGRAMS FOR WEIGHT LOSS**

	80/20 PROGRAM	**HIGH-INTENSITY INTERVALS PROGRAM**
MONDAY		High-Intensity Intervals 5:00 warm-up 6 x (1:00 high intensity/2:00 low intensity) 5:00 cool-down
TUESDAY	Easy Run 40:00 low intensity	
WEDNESDAY	High-Intensity Intervals 5:00 warm-up 6 x (1:00 high intensity/2:00 low intensity) 5:00 cool-down	High-Intensity Intervals 5:00 warm-up 6 x (1:00 high intensity/2:00 low intensity) 5:00 cool-down
THURSDAY	Easy Run 40:00 low intensity	
FRIDAY	Threshold Run 10:00 low intensity 20:00 moderate intensity 10:00 low intensity	High-Intensity Intervals 5:00 warm-up 6 x (1:00 high intensity/2:00 low intensity) 5:00 cool-down
SATURDAY	Easy Run 40:00 low intensity	
SUNDAY	Long Run 60:00 low intensity	High-Intensity Intervals 5:00 warm-up 6 x (1:00 high intensity/2:00 low intensity) 5:00 cool-down
TOTAL PERCEIVED EFFORT	1,032	1,008
TOTAL CALORIES BURNED (assumes a 160-lb runner)	3,075	1,461

trainer's supervision. But I've met scores of people who have fallen in love with running and have lost weight almost as a side effect of training for 5Ks, 10Ks, half marathons, and marathons. Even these runners could do better, though, in many cases. As I've already dem-onstrated, nearly all recreational runners spend too much time run-ning at moderate intensity, day after day making the same compromise between the desire to get their run over with quickly and the desire not to suffer. The few who follow the 80/20 Rule tend to lose the greatest amount of weight most readily.

One such runner is Amanda from Richmond, Virginia. Amanda kept her body lean and fit through athletics in high school, but then she quit sports in college and gained weight—and then she met her husband, Michael, and gained some more. When she was thirty years old, Amanda reached a new peak weight of 195 pounds, and she decided enough was enough. Completely inactive at the time, Amanda started to use strength workout videos at home and to do very short runs of a mile or so around her neighborhood. At the same time, she made sensible changes to her diet, such as cutting out soft drinks, cooking with less meat and more vegetables, and eating out less often.

Amanda had been running for a few months and had com-pleted two 5Ks and one 10K when she discovered PEAR Mobile, the heart rate–based coaching app that I first mentioned in the Introduction. She used my Level 1 Half Marathon program, which is based on the 80/20 Rule, to train for her first 13.1 miler. As most runners do when they are first exposed to this way of training, Amanda discovered that she was forced to run a lot slower (as much as two minutes per mile slower) than she was accustomed to doing.

At first, she resisted being held back, doubting that such easy jogging could do her much good. But before long, Amanda em-braced the program because it freed her from the disappoint-ment she had always felt when training by pace and setting time goals that she couldn't achieve. Training became more enjoyable than ever, and her progress accelerated. Running only a few miles was a struggle for Amanda when she started the program, but when it was over, she finished her half marathon with ease, beating her goal time by four minutes.

Ten months after she started her 80/20 running journey, Amanda stepped on a scale and saw that she weighed 145 pounds. She had lost an even fifty pounds since the start of her new chapter in life. As impressive as Amanda's turnaround is, there are countless others just like it. If you need to lose weight and you commit to 80/20 running, you will end up with a similar story to tell.

The Level 1 5K Plan presented in chapter 9 is a good choice for beginning runners who are seeking to lose weight. Although the plan was designed to prepare new runners to complete their first 5K event, I wouldn't have made the schedule any different if I had created it expressly to promote weight loss. In fact, I encourage people who take up running for the sake of losing weight to set a goal of completing a 5K or some other short event instead of focusing solely on weight-related goals. Research in the field of exercise psychology has demonstrated that people tend to be more motivated by social goals like finishing a race than they are by private goals like reaching a certain weight. Preparing for a running event is also a more reliable way to fall in love with running. There's a special magic in the feeling of crossing a finish line for the first time that hooks new runners on the sport.

80/20 TRIATHLON

In 2010, Stuart Galloway and two fellow exercise scientists at the University of Stirling, Scotland, conducted an ambitious study involving recreational triathletes. For six months, Galloway's team monitored the training of ten members of a local triathlon club as they prepared for an Ironman event (2.4-mile swim, 112-mile bike, 26.2-mile run). The athletes were not coached by the scientists themselves but instead were self-guided. Heart rate monitors and perceived effort ratings were used to determine how much time the athletes spent at low, moderate, and high intensity in each discipline. Before the study period began and at various points throughout it, the athletes underwent fitness testing in all three disciplines to determine how well they were responding to their training.

It turned out that, on average, the athletes spent 69 percent of their total Ironman training time at low intensity, 25 percent at moderate intensity, and 6 percent at high intensity. That's better than most recreational runners do, probably because the volume of training the triathletes did was relatively high. The subjects logged upward of eleven hours per week at the height of their Ironman preparations. But 69 percent is still well below the optimal 80 percent of total training time that endurance athletes should spend at low intensity. You may recall that Jonathan Esteve-Lanao's work has shown that runners who spend 80 percent of their training time at low intensity improve significantly more than do runners who spend 65 percent of their training time at low intensity.

Perhaps it's not surprising, then, that the participants in Galloway's study showed little improvement in fitness over the six-month period in which they were monitored. Among the fitness tests that the athletes were subjected to periodically were ones that measured their swimming pace, cycling-power output, and running pace at lactate threshold intensity—tests that are known to be excellent predictors of performance in actual races. On average, the subjects' swimming pace at lactate threshold intensity increased by a trivial 0.7 percent. Their cycling power at the lactate threshold increased by a greater amount—3.3 percent—but this effect was also classified as statistically trivial. Running performance improved the most. The subjects' lactate threshold running pace increased by 7.8 percent over six months. This effect was classified as moderate. Interestingly, the subjects came closest to heeding the 80/20 Rule in their run training, doing 74 percent of their total running at low intensity.

Galloway and his colleagues concluded that the athletes would have been better off doing 80 percent of their training at low intensity in all three disciplines. A subsequent study conducted by our friends Stephen Seiler and Jonathan Esteve-Lanao supported this conclusion. The design was similar to Galloway's. Nine recreational triathletes were monitored over a long period of time as they trained independently for an Ironman event. But on this occasion, the amount of time that the individual athletes spent in each intensity zone was correlated with actual performance in the race. As expected, there was a significant inverse correlation between low-intensity training time and race time. Athletes got twice as much benefit from each additional minute of low-intensity training in their program as they got from each additional minute of high-intensity training.

The take-home lesson is that if you ever decide to branch out from running to the triathlon, you should be sure to avoid the mistake that most triathletes make and follow the 80/20 Rule. The five-zone intensity scheme that you use for running may also be applied to your swimming and cycling. However, because the lactate threshold heart rate is different for each activity, you will need to establish distinct training zones for swimming, cycling, and running. You can determine your cycling lactate threshold heart rate and power output (if your bike has a power meter) by using the same test you use for running, whether it's a thirty-minute time trial, a perceived effort test, or the talk test.

The best way to find your lactate threshold pace in the water is with something called the *critical velocity test*. It's fairly simple: Go to the pool, warm up with some easy swimming, and then swim four hundred yards as fast as you can, recording your time. Rest for several minutes and then swim two hundred yards as fast as you can, again recording your time. Use the following formula to calculate your critical velocity, which is also your lactate threshold swim pace.

$$\text{Critical velocity} = (400 \text{ yards} - 200 \text{ yards}) \div (400 \text{ time} - 200 \text{ time})$$

Let's look at an example. Suppose you swim your four-hundred-yard test in 4:21 (4.35 minutes) and your two-hundred-yard test in 2:02 (2.04 minutes). Your critical velocity, then, is (400y −

200y) ÷ (4.35 min. – 2.02 min.) = 86.6 yards/min. It is customary to express critical speed in the form of time per hundred yards. To make this conversion, divide one hundred by your critical velocity. In this example, 100 ÷ 86.6 = 1.15. So your lactate threshold pace per hundred yards is 1.15 minutes, or 1 minute and 9 seconds (which is really fast, by the way).

You can determine your swimming lactate threshold heart rate by swimming several laps at your lactate threshold pace and then pausing to check your heart rate. Although there are some heart rate monitors that work in the water, most swimmers and triathletes prefer to monitor and control the intensity of their swim workouts by pace because it's almost impossible to check one's heart rate while swimming freestyle. Table 13.1 shows appropriate swim pace targets for the five-zone intensity scheme.

TABLE 13.1 **SWIMMING PACE ZONES**

ZONE	PACE RANGE (AS PERCENTAGE OF CRITICAL VELOCITY/ LACTATE THRESHOLD SPEED)
1	80–85
2	86–90
3	96–100
4	103–106
5	>107

Perceived effort may be used to monitor intensity in cycling and swimming just as it is in running. In all three disciplines, Zone 1 corresponds to ratings of 1–2, Zone 2 to ratings of 3–4, Zone 3 to ratings of 5–6, Zone 4 to ratings of 7–8, and Zone 5 to ratings of 9–10.

Following is a twelve-week 80/20 training plan that you can follow to prepare for your first Olympic-distance triathlon (0.93-mile swim, 24.8-mile bike, 6.2-mile run) or use as a template to design your own 80/20 triathlon plan. The run workout codes refer to those presented in chapter 7.

	MON	TUE	WED	THU	FRI	SAT	SUN
1		Swim 600 yards w/ 4 x 50 Z5	Bike 30:00 w/ 4 x 1:00 Z4	Speed Play Run 2	Swim 600 yards Z1/Z2	Bike 45:00 w/ 10:00 Z3	Foundation Run 6
2		Swim 700 yards w/ 5 x 50 Z5	Bike 35:00 w/ 4 x 1:00 Z5	Speed Play Run 3	Swim 700 yards Z1/Z2	Bike 50:00 w/ 10:00 Z3	Foundation Run 7
3		Swim 600 yards w/ 4 x 50 Z5	Bike 30:00 w/ 4 x 1:00 Z4	Speed Play Run 2	Swim 600 yards Z1/Z2	Bike 45:00 w/ 10:00 Z3	Foundation Run 6
4		Swim 800 yards w/ 3 x 100 Z4	Bike 40:00 Z1/Z2	Hill Repetition Run 4	Swim 800 yards Z1/Z2	Bike 55:00 w/ 3 x 3:00 uphill Z4	Foundation Run 9
5		Swim 1,000 yards w/ 4 x 100 Z4	Bike 45:00 w/ 15:00 Z3	Hill Repetition Run 6	Swim 1,000 yards Z1/Z2	Bike 60:00 Z1/Z2 + 10:00 Run Z2	Long Run 2
6		Swim 800 yards w/ 6 x 50 Z4	Bike 40:00 w/ 3 x 3:00 uphill Z4	Speed Play Run 3	Swim 800 yards Z1/Z2	Bike 50:00 Z1/Z2	Foundation Run 7
7		Swim 1,250 yards w/ 5 x 100 Z4	Bike 48:00 w/ 18:00 Z3	Long Interval Run 3	Swim 1,250 yards Z1/Z2	Bike 65:00 Z1/Z2 + 10:00 Run Z2	Long Run 3
8		Swim 1,500 yards w/ 3 x 200 Z3	Bike 50:00 w/ 8 x 1:00 Z5	Long Interval Run 5	Swim 1,500 yards Z1/Z2	Bike 70:00 Z1/Z2 + 10:00 Run Z2	Long Run 4
9		Swim 1,000 yards w/ 4 x 100 Z4	Bike 45:00 w/ 15:00 Z3	Tempo Run 1	Swim 1,000 yards Z1/Z2	Bike 60:00 Z1/Z2	Foundation Run 8

	MON	TUE	WED	THU	FRI	SAT	SUN
10		Swim 1,750 yards w/ 5 x 150 Z3	Bike 50:00 w/ 20:00 Z3	Tempo Run 2	Swim 1,750 yards Z1/Z2	Bike 75:00 Z1/Z2 + 5:00 Run Z3	Long Run 5
11		Swim 2,000 yards w/ 4 x 200 Z3	Bike 45:00 w/ 3 x 5:00 Z4	Tempo Run 3	Swim 2,000 yards Z1/Z2	Bike 80:00 Z1/Z2	Long Run 3
12		Swim 1,500 yards w/ 3 x 200 Z3	Bike 45:00 w/ 15:00 Z3	Fast Finish Run 4	Swim 1,000 yards Z1/Z2		Triathlon

THE LIMITS OF 80/20

Running is not a lifelong sport for everyone. Many passionate runners either choose or are forced to trade running for gentler activities such as cycling and swimming because of age or injury. My father, for example, had a hip replaced in his late fifties and subsequently traded his decades-old running habit for open-water swimming, which had been the sport of his youth.

If there should ever come a time when you want or need to make a similar switch, and you wish to get the best possible results from your new endurance sport, whatever it may be, then be sure to take the 80/20 Rule with you. As we saw in chapter 3, elite athletes in all endurance sports—including cross-country skiing, cycling, rowing, and swimming—heed this rule because it works better than any alternative. Controlled studies suggest that an 80/20 training intensity distribution is optimal for recreational athletes in these other sports as well. In a 2013 study, for example, Stuart Galloway found that six weeks of 80/20 training increased high-intensity endurance capacity in cyclists by 85 percent, whereas six weeks of 57/43 training resulted in a much smaller 37 percent increase.

Arthur Lydiard, the man who developed the low-intensity, high-volume approach to training on which the 80/20 method is based, believed it was the best method of cardiovascular conditioning even in nonendurance sports such as football and track sprinting. Low-intensity, high-volume training was his hammer and every sport under the sun looked like a nail. But it was a bridge too far. Elite athletes in strength, speed, and power sports today base their training on high-intensity workouts that simulate the specific demands of their sports, and studies confirm that this approach works best for them.

Lydiard was not omniscient. He made the most important training discovery in the history of running, which led directly to the most important breakthrough since then—namely, Stephen Seiler's identification of the 80/20 Rule—but he had no business telling wrestlers and the like how to train. So, if someday you give up running in favor of, say, ice hockey, leave behind the 80/20 Rule without a second thought and train the way the best hockey players train.

There are few absolute principles in life, and the 80/20 Rule is not one of them. It is nothing more than the solution to the single most common training mistake in running and the key to becoming the best, most fulfilled runner you can possibly be.

APPENDIX

DETAILED INTENSITY CONTROL GUIDELINES FOR 80/20 WORKOUTS

The following table presents step-by-step instructions on how to monitor and control intensity in each type of run based on the principles described in chapter 6.

LOW-INTENSITY RUNS	
Recovery Run	• Use perceived effort (1–2) to establish Zone 1 intensity.
	• Use heart rate to stay in Zone 1.
	• Use perceived effort to fine-tune your effort as necessary through the entire workout.
Foundation Run	• Use perceived effort (1–2) to establish Zone 1 intensity in the warm-up.
	• Use heart rate to stay in Zone 1 through completion of the warm-up.
	• Use perceived effort (3–4) to make the initial adjustment to Zone 2 after warm-up.
	• Use heart rate to stay in Zone 2 throughout the Zone 2 segment of the run.
	• Use perceived effort (1–2) to make the initial adjustment to Zone 1 for the cool-down.
	• Use heart rate to stay in Zone 1 throughout the cool-down.
	• Use perceived effort to fine-tune your effort as necessary through the entire workout.
Long Run	• Same as Foundation Run.
MODERATE-INTENSITY RUNS	
Fast Finish Run	• Use perceived effort (1–2) to establish Zone 1 intensity in the warm-up.

(continued)

Fast Finish Run (continued)	• Use heart rate to stay in Zone 1 through completion of the warm-up.
	• Use perceived effort (3–4) to make the initial adjustment to Zone 2 after the warm-up.
	• Use heart rate to stay in Zone 2 throughout the Zone 2 segment of the run.
	• Use perceived effort (5–6) to make the initial adjustment to Zone 3 for the fast finish.
	• Use pace, heart rate, or both to maintain Zone 3 intensity until the end of the run.
	• Use perceived effort to fine-tune your effort as necessary through the entire workout.
Tempo Run	• Use perceived effort (1–2) to establish Zone 1 intensity in the warm-up.
	• Use heart rate to stay in Zone 1 through completion of the warm-up.
	• Use perceived effort (3–4) to make the initial adjustment to Zone 2 after the warm-up.
	• Use heart rate to stay in Zone 2 throughout the Zone 2 segment of the run.
	• Use perceived effort (5–6) to make the initial adjustment to Zone 3 for the tempo portion of the run.
	• Use pace, heart rate, or both to maintain Zone 3 intensity throughout the tempo portion of the run.
	• Use perceived effort to make the initial adjustments back to Zone 2 and finally Zone 1 for the cool-down.
	• Use heart rate to stay in Zone 2 and finally Zone 1 for the last two steps of the workout.
	• Use perceived effort to fine-tune your effort as necessary through the entire workout.
Cruise Interval Run	• Use perceived effort (1–2) to establish Zone 1 intensity in the warm-up.
	• Use heart rate to stay in Zone 1 through completion of the warm-up.
	• Use perceived effort (3–4) to make the initial adjustment to Zone 2 after the warm-up.
	• Use heart rate to stay in Zone 2 throughout the Zone 2 segment of the run.
	• Use perceived effort (5–6) to make the initial adjustment to Zone 3 for each cruise interval.
	• Use pace, heart rate, or both to maintain Zone 3 intensity throughout each cruise interval.

Cruise Interval Run	• Use perceived effort to make the initial adjustment back to Zone 2 after each cruise interval.
	• Use heart rate to stay in Zone 2 throughout each recovery period between cruise intervals.
	• Use perceived effort to make the initial adjustments back to Zone 2 and finally Zone 1 for the cool-down.
	• Use heart rate to stay in Zone 2 and finally Zone 1 for the last two steps of the workout.
	• Use perceived effort to fine-tune your effort as necessary through the entire workout.
Long Run with Speed Play	• Same as Cruise Interval Run, except time-based cruise intervals are replaced with distance-based speed-play segments
Long Run with Fast Finish	• Same as Fast Finish Run.

HIGH-INTENSITY RUNS

Speed Play Run	• Use perceived effort (1–2) to establish Zone 1 intensity in the warm-up.
	• Use heart rate to stay in Zone 1 through completion of the warm-up.
	• Use perceived effort (3–4) to make the initial adjustment to Zone 2 after the warm-up.
	• Use heart rate to stay in Zone 2 throughout the Zone 2 segment of the run.
	• Use perceived effort to make the initial adjustment to *either* Zone 4 *or* Zone 5 for each speed play segment. Choose an initial RPE of 7 for Zone 4 speed play segments and 9 for Zone 5 speed-play segments.
	• Use RPE to maintain Zone 4 or Zone 5 intensity throughout each speed play segment. RPE may climb from 7 to 8 in Zone 4 speed play segments, but as a general rule it should not reach 8 until you're at least halfway through the workout. Likewise, RPE may climb from 9 to 10 in Zone 5 speed play segments, but as a general rule, it should not reach 10 until you're at least halfway through the workout.
	• Use perceived effort (3–4) to make the initial adjustment to Zone 2 after each speed play segment.
	• Use heart rate to stay in Zone 2 throughout each recovery period between speed play segments.
	• Use perceived effort (1–2) to make the initial adjustment to Zone 1 for the cool-down.
	• Use heart rate to stay in Zone 1 throughout cool-down.

(continued)

Speed Play Run (continued)	• Use perceived effort to fine-tune your effort as necessary through the entire workout. **Note:** If you choose to employ Greg McMillan's pace guidelines for Speed Play Runs, use his recommended Speed Pace for 1200-meter intervals in workouts featuring two-minute efforts in Zone 4 and use his recommended Speed Pace for 400-meter intervals in workouts featuring one-minute efforts in Zone 5.
Hill Repetition Run	• Use perceived effort (1–2) to establish Zone 1 intensity in the warm-up. • Use heart rate to stay in Zone 1 through completion of the warm-up. • Use perceived effort (3–4) to make the initial adjustment to Zone 2 after the warm-up. • Use heart rate to stay in Zone 2 throughout the Zone 2 segment of the run. • Use perceived effort (5–6) to make the initial adjustment to Zone 5 for each speed play segment. • Use pace to stay in either Zone 4 or Zone 5 throughout each speed play segment. • Use perceived effort (1–2) to make the initial adjustment to Zone 1 after each speed play segment. • Use perceived effort to stay in Zone 1 throughout each recovery period between hill repetitions. • Use perceived effort (1–2) to make the initial adjustment to Zone 1 for the cool-down. • Use heart rate to stay in Zone 1 throughout the cool-down. • Use perceived effort to fine-tune your effort as necessary through the entire workout.
Short Interval Run	• Use perceived effort (1–2) to establish Zone 1 intensity in the warm-up. • Use heart rate to stay in Zone 1 through completion of the warm-up. • Use perceived effort (3-4) to make the initial adjustment to Zone 2 after the warm-up. • Use heart rate to stay in Zone 2 throughout the Zone 2 segment of run. • Use perceived effort (9) to make the initial adjustment to Zone 5 at the start of each Short Interval. • Use pace to stay in Zone 5 through the end of each Short Interval. • Use perceived effort (1–2) to make the initial adjustment to Zone 1 after completing each Short Interval.

Short Interval Run	• Use perceived effort to stay in Zone 1 throughout each recovery period between Short Intervals.
	• Use perceived effort (1–2) to make the initial adjustment to Zone 1 for the cool-down.
	• Use heart rate to stay in Zone 1 throughout the cool-down.
	• Use perceived effort to fine-tune your effort as necessary through the entire workout.
	Note: If you choose to employ Greg McMillan's pace guidelines for Short Interval Runs, use his recommended Speed Pace for 400-meter intervals in workouts featuring one-minute intervals and use his recommended Speed Pace for 600-meter intervals in workouts featuring 1.5-minute efforts in Zone 5.
Long Interval Run	• Use perceived effort (1–2) to establish Zone 1 intensity in the warm-up.
	• Use heart rate to stay in Zone 1 through completion of the warm-up.
	• Use perceived effort (3–4) to make the initial adjustment to Zone 2 after the warm-up.
	• Use heart rate to stay in Zone 2 throughout the Zone 2 segment of the run.
	• Use perceived effort (7) to make the initial adjustment to Zone 4 at the start of each Long Interval.
	• Use pace to stay in Zone 4 through the end of each Long Interval.
	• Use perceived effort (1–2) to make the initial adjustment to Zone 1 after completing each Long Interval.
	• Use perceived effort to stay in Zone 1 throughout each recovery period between Long Intervals.
	• Use perceived effort (1–2) to make the initial adjustment to Zone 1 for the cool-down.
	• Use heart rate to stay in Zone 1 throughout the cool-down.
	• Use perceived effort to fine-tune your effort as necessary through the entire workout.
	Note: If you choose to employ Greg McMillan's pace guidelines for Long Interval Runs, use his recommended Speed Pace for 1000-meter intervals in workouts featuring three-minute intervals and use his recommended Speed Pace for 1200-meter intervals in workouts featuring five-minute intervals.

(continued)

Mixed Interval Run	• Use perceived effort (1–2) to establish Zone 1 intensity in the warm-up.
	• Use heart rate to stay in Zone 1 through completion of the warm-up.
	• Use perceived effort (3–4) to make the initial adjustment to Zone 2 after the warm-up.
	• Use heart rate to stay in Zone 2 throughout the Zone 2 segment of run.
	• Use perceived effort (9) to make the initial adjustment to Zone 5 at the start of each Zone 5 interval.
	• Use pace to stay in Zone 5 through the end of each Zone 5 interval.
	• Use perceived effort (7) to make the initial adjustment to Zone 5 at the start of each Zone 4 interval.
	• Use pace to stay in Zone 4 through the end of each Zone 4 interval.
	• Use perceived effort (5–6) to make the initial adjustment to Zone 3 at the start of the Zone 3 interval(s).
	• Use heart rate, pace, or both to stay in Zone 3 through the end of the Zone 3 interval(s).
	• Use perceived effort (1–2) to make the initial adjustment to Zone 1 after completing each interval.
	• Use perceived effort to stay in Zone 1 throughout each recovery period between intervals.
	• Use perceived effort (1–2) to make the initial adjustment to Zone 1 for the cool-down.
	• Use heart rate to stay in Zone 1 throughout the cool-down.
	• Use perceived effort to fine-tune your effort as necessary through the entire workout.
	Note: If you choose to employ Greg McMillan's pace guidelines for Mixed Interval Runs, use his recommended Speed Pace for 1200-meter intervals in workouts featuring three-minute efforts in Zone 4, use his recommended Speed Pace for 1600-meter intervals in workouts featuring five-minute efforts in Zone 4, use his recommended Speed Pace for 400-meter intervals in workouts featuring one-minute efforts in Zone 5, and use his recommended Speed Pace for 600-meter intervals in workouts featuring 1.5-minute efforts in Zone 5.

INDEX

MATT FITZGERALD is an acclaimed endurance sports and nutrition writer and certified sports nutritionist. He is the author of the bestselling *Racing Weight,* and has ghostwritten for sports celebrities including Dean Karnazes and Kara Goucher. Fitzgerald is a columnist on Competitor.com and Active.com, and has contributed to *Bicycling, Men's Health, Triathlete, Men's Journal, Outside, Runner's World, Shape,* and *Women's Health.*